BECOMING

Meditations for the Ministry Minded

By Mae D. Williams

Becoming
by Mae D. Williams

Printed in the United States of America

ISBN 1-60034-544-1

Unless otherwise indicated, Bible quotations are taken from the New International Version of the Bible. Copyright 1973, 1978, © 1984 by Zondervan.

www.xulonpress.com

Contents

"Therefore, since we have this ministry, as we have received mercy, we do not lose heart, but we have renounced the things hidden because of shame, not walking in craftiness or adulterating the Word of God, but by manifestation of truth commending ourselves to every man's conscience in the sight of God." —2 Corinthians 4:1-2

Prologue

I acknowledged my call into ministry at the age of
fourteen. It was during a time of searching. I had
a desire to understand the Word of God since I came
to know Jesus as my Savior at ten years old. Before
my conversion, I had listened to sermons. Some parts
made sense to me; others did not. Probably because
of my youth, I became lost in the odd language of the
Bible with all the references to *thee, thou,* and *thus*
and the unusual usages for words that made the text
nearly indecipherable to me.

I believe God hears the heart of a child. I am
thankful for my parents, who provided an understandable set of Bible storybooks for my siblings and me.
They sat on the bookshelf for a few years, but by the
beginning of high school I began to devour them. I
carried them everywhere with me and read whenever I
had the chance. After I finished the books, I was better
able to understand what was occurring in the Bible as
well as the connections between the Scriptures.

Attendance at training institutes for ministers at
church conventions confirmed what the Holy Spirit

was teaching me in terms of homiletics and herme-neutics. By the time I began preaching at fifteen, my understanding astounded my elders.

Since that time I have served in many capaci-ties in church settings, each of which has been an exciting learning experience for me and, I hope, a blessing to the congregation. I have periodically been called upon to discuss issues of maturity in Christ. I believe part of the reason for this interest in the Word of God through me is due to the transparency of my life before believers and the unsaved. As a young Christian woman minister, I have grown up in the presence of the church. I dated, got married, had chil-dren, and raised teenagers in the sight of the people of God. The Lord has blessed me to go through some of the same issues others are confronting. Some of these experiences have had less than flattering results, yet God has sustained my faith.

People often approach me and ask how I did it. My most accurate response is that God urged me to pray to Him during this time. I've been frustrated, confused, and have made mistakes along the way, but the conviction of His Word helped me understand much of what I had to do. This conviction sometimes came through hearing the preached Word, at group Bible studies, in spiritual songs and hymns, through personal meditation on His Word, through conver-sations with fellow laborers, and through "remem-brances," which I believe came from the Holy Spirit.

As I pondered my walk in ministry, I always felt a sense of being "different," of not seeing life from the same perspectives as my contemporaries. This sense became an acute desire to mentor those who were studying for ministry in our church.

My first charges were eight dynamic, dedicated women. Our task together was to study, pray, and engage in deep discussions about what it means to be in ministry, both in conduct and in inner life. This ended after four years as they began their own public ministries.

This experience led me to a great sense of responsibility for being the watcher and encourager of ministers. Much of what is written herein was originally penned with aspiring ministers in mind. These are some of the thoughts that I believe must be deeply owned as one enters into and continues in ministry.

Why a Book for Ministers about Ministry?

In 2004, over the period of one year, I took a survey of people operating in the ministry and found that many believe there is a need for books to encourage them in their walk. As servants, ministers have made the commitment to be available to God for whatever He bids them to accomplish. However, ministers have the same needs as anyone else, which include the basic human requirements as well as the fellowship of a community of others who understand, support, and affirm them.

The ministers I spoke to emphasized the need for a book that reminds them of their relationship with God and all of its ramifications. Even in times of great discouragement, we must continue the walk. Sometimes that walk is solitary, and no earthly person understands it. Sometimes not even the minister understands. The standard set for ministers by God and a watching world is high. After all, we represent the Father to the world's hurting, dying people. We also bring hope and encouragement to God's people. People expect that they can trust us.

As a result of media reports of the immoral acts of some people in ministry, the world is watching us very carefully. Now more than ever they ask why they should trust anything a man or woman of God says. Even ministers who have not been caught in this kind of trouble are looked upon with distrust and scrutiny. This may not change the way a minister walks, but it should make us more aware of the need for circumspection. It humbles us and reminds us of our sinful nature, yet it also makes us want to live up to the ideals of our heavenly Father and our trusting parishioners. It is my hope that this book will serve as a tool that Christian ministers can use to examine their lives and enter into deep communion with the Father.

After sharing this work with others who are already in Christian ministry, I realized it would not only serve as a meditative aid for those entering, but also as a reminder to those already knee-deep in ministry, who may be struggling with issues of uncertainty or strength, confidence or peace, or are just too busy.

Those of us who are no longer new to ministry still pray, but our prayers may have ceased to have undertones of adoration and exaltation, and may instead have become hurried requests for help in one endeavor or another. At some point in our lives all ministers grapple with the issue of being leaders of people and followers of God. So, God calls us closer to Him for periods of refreshing if we will hear Him. Going through this experience makes us grow deeper in our love for Him, to become more like our Savior. However, getting stuck in activities without heeding his call can be deadly to our own faith.

This book is meant to help those who are in the throes of doing so much in the name of Christ that they are in danger of losing touch with the One for whom they work so hard. My intention is not to encourage laziness or to cast a critical eye upon the industrious. This book is a call to greater intimacy with the Master, a call to communion and renewal with the One who loves you most. Just as Jesus went into the mountains to pray, He bids you to come aside awhile and rest.

How to Use this Book

As a minister of the gospel, I have been around ministers all my life, and I am convinced that we neglect our own spiritual growth as often as mothers neglect themselves in order to care for their children. Sometimes, even though we are hungry, we feed everyone else and leave ourselves out completely. I have heard that when a family member becomes ill, the caretaker usually dies first, not the person with the debilitating condition. In much the same way ministers, working for others without respite, are in danger of spiritual, emotional, psychological, and physical death. Others may appear to be benefiting from our ministry, but we are sliding into a state of uselessness if we do not stop to accept renewal for ourselves.

The apostle Paul compared staying in spiritual shape to the preparation of a fighter. "But [like a boxer] I buffet my body [handle it roughly, discipline it by hardships] and subdue it, for fear that after proclaiming to others the gospel and things pertaining to it, I myself should become unfit [not stand the test, be unapproved and rejected as a counterfeit]."[1] Becoming ineffective is the last thing any minister wants. So I encourage you to read, meditate, and receive.

This book is meant to serve as an aid in a minister's times of meditation. This can take place daily, whether in the early morning before the day's activities begin, while admiring a beautiful sunrise, or at day's end when you worship God for the work He has accomplished. I suggest each section be read and meditated upon and that the questions at the end of each chapter are honestly answered in prayer to the Father.

The book is divided into four major parts. In Part I, you are invited to reminisce about the beginning of the journey and to remember how sweetly you were called away from the distractions of secular life to the Christian life. Part II invites you to call to mind how God is showing Himself in your life and the resultant maturity, whether in small or major life areas. In Part III, you are invited to explore the ramifications of complete surrender to the will of Christ in worship, in healing, and in life. Part IV invites you to delve into a deeper relationship with the Master by watching His miraculous work, releasing old weights that have served as distractions so that you and I are able to move into new places of greater depth in Him.

At the conclusion of each chapter are questions to ponder. You are encouraged to write your heart thoughts in a journal. This would allow you to document your spiritual growth over time, which will in turn assist the congregation you serve in their spiritual growth.

It is my sincere hope that you will take this book as a hiatus that will spur spiritual renewal in the name of Christ Jesus. Amen.

PART I

Once in Darkness

Part I – Introduction

One day as I sat conversing with a group of aspiring ministers about the call on our lives, the conversation came to a discussion of how and when we first came to know Jesus as our Savior. This is a fundamental issue, for how do you bring a message to the hearts of people from the heart and mind of Someone you have never met? During the discourse each of us discovered we had not met Him in the same way. He had come for us at different times in our lives and through different experiences. Though we did not have a common method, we all had a personal meeting with the Father through His Son, Jesus.

For some of us, a realization came after an event that caused us to understand the brevity of our lives and the need to be grounded in God. Joan, for example, was brought up in church as a child. She recounted a day when she was driving home from college to attend her grandmother's funeral. Her grandmother's death had enhanced her thoughts of her own eternal destiny. As she rounded a curve that displayed the beautiful Blue Ridge Mountains on the Virginia skyline, something about the transcendence of that scene gave new revelation to her belief system. At that moment, she came to the realization that she indeed believed in Jesus as her Savior and heaven was her eternal destination.

Others of us made a conscious decision to repeat a prayer that echoed the essence of our desire to be connected to God. Such was the case for Dee, who lived next door to a church while growing up and had a certain cynicism for its members because she saw some of them looking pious on Sunday morning after having spent the previous evening at an after-hours club. Dee remembered going to church as an adult with a relative. She was drawn to the preaching and went forward at the minister's invitation to receive Christ as her Savior.

These stories and others indicated there was a definite time when we were unaware of the saving grace offered to us by God. Some of us were taught it from the time we are born. Others had never heard of the unconditional love of God. Still others thought we needed to get ourselves into shape before going to church. Some of us, when trying to address our heavenly Father, became so frustrated in trying to put together the right words that we gave up until something or someone touched our hearts. Whatever our previous paths—whether lack of knowledge, lack of understanding, or lack of connectedness to God—we were in darkness. When we came out of the darkness and into the light, we had the privilege of coming to the profound realization that we did not reach this point on our own. The love of God was extended to us long before we knew about it. We needed Him to be merciful to us in the state in which we were found.

The three discourses in this section challenge us to ponder our own journey in understanding that there is a destiny beyond what we may accomplish on earth. We do not reach this destiny totally of our own accord. Our heavenly Father is constantly at work to bring us to that point.

Chapter 1

Down Memory Lane

When she was six, my youngest daughter said to me one day, "What's the point?" I stared at her. The question seemed to come out of nowhere. I couldn't recall having had any deep conversations with her. I gave her a perplexed look. She spread her little arms much like an adult would when pondering the meaning of life and said, "I mean, what is the point of living?"

Many of us seem to be born running toward our destiny. It is as if we have a computer inside that has been preprogrammed to play, fight, sing, write, or whatever. Yet if we had the capacity to examine the true motivations of others, we might find that, more often than not, people are just doing what they believe they are supposed to do at different points in their lives—going to school, graduating, getting a job. Many of us never take the time to question the reason for our existence, even though this is a fundamental question that every human being should answer.

Other people seem to go through their lives like aimless shoppers, trying on various identities, looking for their life's purpose. Sadly, some run so long without paying attention to what is occurring internally that they do not find their destinies before their lives end. They never realized the real destiny was Jesus.

For those of us who are actively attending to the Father's pursuit of us, we came to Jesus like sea turtles born on land that find their way back to the water. Our lives were in a wretched state, and we were aware of our need for someone or something to give us peace with our heavenly Father. Others of us were happy overall, but sensed that something was missing. At the time we may not have known it, but we were searching for God. According to the apostle Paul, our lives were distant from the Father, and we were in darkness.

The Meaning of Darkness

Darkness implies the burden of sin and the inability to see or be seen. We were ignorant of the state in which we were living. Scripture speaks of the groping that goes on in darkness for lack of sight.[1] I would venture to say during that time we also lacked *insight*. At one point we even relished in the dark, for Jesus said, "Men love darkness, for their deeds are evil."[2]

We were in a terrible state, separated from God, and we loved it. We did not know how bad we were. We were not aware that if we had died in that state, we would have "lifted up our eyes in hell."[3] Yet those who looked to us for guidance and leadership were following, perhaps even admiring the ways in which we were able to "get ahead, get by, get even," and even "get over" in various types of situations. We were leading our own admirers to hell as well.

The apostle Paul described himself as the chief sinner because he persecuted the church.[4] In the Acts of the Apostles, he is described as consenting to the death of Stephen the deacon,[5] even holding his garment while others stoned him.[6] As a member of the Sanhedrin, and with permission from the officials of the Jewish temple, he had set out to cleanse the temple of these insurgents called Christians.

As a scribe, Paul (then known as Saul) must have been particularly angered at these people who continually gathered in the temple, teaching and encouraging others to accept Jesus as Messiah. It must have infuriated him to see Israel being turned upside down by these ignorant and uneducated men who seemed to possess such charisma. In the past, the temple leaders had successfully turned away others claiming to be the Messiah.

The Turning Point

These followers of Christ raised some questions that could not be easily dismissed. The displays of their faith must have given the Jewish high priests the disconcerting sense that the temple would change forever if these people weren't stopped. They performed healing and other miracles. How? What about the authority with which Jesus spoke, as if He had heard from the very mouth of the Almighty? Now these men spoke by the authority of Jesus.

Given the account of the discussion between the two men on the road to Emmaus,[7] it is evident that widespread conversations about the resurrection of Jesus took place. The skeptics tried to dismiss it by saying His disciples probably attacked the soldiers, pushed away the stone, and carried His body away. However, this rumor did not hold water, especially since so many people saw Jesus alive after His resurrection.[8]

Another argument could have been that someone who looked like Him was masquerading as this risen Messiah. Yet how could the scars on his body be so much like those of Jesus?

Maybe He hadn't really been killed on the cross at Golgotha and his devoted followers took Him away and nursed Him to health. But how could His wounds have healed so quickly? After all, the first sighting was only three days after His death, and no one could recover so quickly from the wounds made by nails driven through the hands and feet and a spear through the side.

All this must have eaten away at Saul. According to Acts 9, Jesus Christ used Saul's own intelligence and a supernatural experience to change him forever. So drastic was the change that his name was changed to Paul.

A Personal God

God sometimes has to turn our lives upside down to get our attention. He uses our own strengths and needs to make us curious about Him. God is deliberate in His work of getting our attention.

I was a young girl when I realized I needed Jesus. At ten years old, I made a serious vow to God in a simple prayer. I gave Him my life in exchange for my home.

In the midst of a terrible neighborhood fire that claimed the life of a two-year-old girl, the firemen warned my family that our house would certainly be the next to ignite. I asked God to please save my home and promised that if He did, I would give Him my life in the next revival. Our house was spared and we were back in our own beds by the wee hours of the next morning.

I thought about that vow for a while, but eventually forgot about it...until after I came to know Jesus as my Savior at the very next revival. When I remembered I laughed with the satisfaction that even though I might forget because of my own human frailties, God didn't forget. He came to collect what was already dedicated to Him. He came for me.

What was your experience? I invite you to take a moment to remember what you were like when you were in darkness. Remember the emptiness, the sense that something was missing, or the utter desire with which you lived before you finally yielded to the Holy Spirit's call. Remember the distance you came since you came into the light.

Points to Ponder

1. What was your life like before you came to Christ?

2. What would your life be like now had you not come to know Christ as Savior?

Chapter 2

When the Moment of Truth Arrives

In the midst of my busy life I needed You.
After all of my accomplishments, I needed
    You.
When I tried to make sense of life, and there
    was none,
In the final analysis, all I ever needed
    was You.

When I celebrated, the emptiness was
    deafening.
My tongue stuck to the roof of my mouth,
full of the nothingness of life.
Digging deep into my soul for a reason
    to go on,
In the final analysis, all I ever needed
    was You.[1]

My dad, an ordained minister, was a full-time pastor at a small church in New England. The church was unable to financially support his growing family, so he took a welding job. He often found himself in spiritual conversations during lunch or on the way to his car after work.

One day as he was eating his meal, a coworker named Ray began to describe his exploits. He said he had been to the priest to be forgiven of his sins. Dad told Ray he needed more than confession to be right with God. He explained the gospel, describing Christ as our mediator to God. He told him about the power God has to live in and through us in our daily walk. Ray became agitated and upset. "Oh, I am not saved," he exclaimed. "I have been deceived. I need to be saved."

Nothing Dad said could detract from the traumatic realization he had on that day. Ray had just realized he was a sinner who needed to repent and that he had no power in himself to come to salvation. He was disappointed with his religious background. Seeing his wretched state, he knew he needed a personal relationship with God.

Accountability

In this time and day there is much to obstruct us from taking responsibility for our wrongdoings. Some believe that people are basically good and that sin is a myth. Others think people are victims of circumstances, that the choices they make are not voluntary, but a natural progression of events. This dismissal of sin as nonexistent or an unfortunate inevitability only postpones what we know in our hearts to be true.

Sometimes the evasion of responsibility takes the form of denial of guilt. We may challenge our accusers to prove that we are guilty and continue to deny our culpability unless indisputable proof is offered. Even then we attempt to explain our guilt away by blaming our depraved upbringing or weakness of mind.

Barring any organic diseases that may attack the mind and render us unable to comprehend our guilt, the greatest relief in the realm of human experience is to admit one's guilt before God and man. Every man carries the burden of guilt from sin until he surrenders to his Maker and comes to true repentance. The shame of having violated God's law is like being naked before the world. It feels like everyone knows your secret and there is nowhere to hide.

The Choice and Its Consequences

The story of the prodigal son[2] is a depiction of the life of mankind from the Garden of Eden to the Savior's death, resurrection, and ascension, and Jesus' ongoing work of salvation. God placed man and woman in this amazing place, giving them everything they needed every day, including fellowship with Him. Yet, for some reason, man was more concerned with what was offered in forbidden places than what God offered and what might be lost by disobedience. So it was with the prodigal son. He had all the comforts of living in his father's house. Even knowing he stood to inherit much upon his father's demise, he decided he could not wait. He demanded his inheritance immediately to spend. He did not consider the consequences of the manner in which he would spend his money. He had no shame for essentially saying to his father with his actions, "I don't want to wait until you die. Who knows, maybe you'll outlive me. I want what is mine now." So he took his inheritance and left, going far away from home and wasting his money "with riotous living."[3]

Even though the circumstances are somewhat different, each of these experiences involves sin and its results. The prodigal son left of his own volition to act out what was already in his heart.

Adam and Eve were not born in sin. But the rest of mankind has been born with sin as our very nature. We cannot help sinning, nor can we control it without a power greater than ourselves. God warned Adam and Eve what would happen if they sinned.[4]

However, the warning was not enough. Thus, God allowed them to taste what it was like to disobey the Father and live with the results.

After having sinned, they were banished from the Garden of Eden. Adam blamed Eve, and Eve blamed the serpent.[5] Neither of them, like the prodigal son before he spent all his money, took personal responsibility for their actions.

Thus, God pronounced judgment upon Adam and Eve, describing the difficulties that lay ahead. This included pain in childbirth, an inordinate attachment of the wife to her husband, difficulties in cultivating the land, and death. As it was with Adam and Eve, so it was with the prodigal son. After having spent all his money, he found himself friendless and hungry. He went to work feeding hogs on a farm until he was so hungry that he was about to eat the slop reserved for livestock.

It is obvious from these two accounts that when man believes he is better without God in his life, the results are disastrous. The depravity of a life of sin, even when covered by the niceties of life, will eventually wear away at the very fiber of one's being.

Many people are deceived by the outward success of those who are accomplished by this world's standards, who take credit for all that they have done or amassed. Regardless of how opulent the lifestyle is, the sinful man is merely avoiding the responsibilities and guilt of his sin. In time, the materialistic facade of apparent success will wear thin, and then the obvious becomes apparent.

In the final analysis, all men will die, whether rich or poor. Jesus said, "What does it profit a man to gain the whole world and lose his soul?"[6]

It's Personal

God gives us opportunities to come to the realization of our need for Him in our own experiences. In the case of Adam and Eve, the realization seemed to come after Cain killed his brother Abel. God gave Adam and Eve another son, whom they called Seth. After Seth grew up and had his own son, "men began to call on the name of the Lord."[7]

The prodigal son, having gone hungry after losing his money, realized his father had much more than he and he would fare better as a servant to his father than on the farm of a stranger. The realization of his state provided the impetus for his move back into his father's presence.

In the church where my father was pastor, I saw people come to the front of the sanctuary to be prayed for after hearing his sermons. I heard stories of the change that came into the lives of people after receiving salvation. I did not understand my own depravity yet, but I hoped Jesus would accept me.

As I sought Him, it seemed difficult to find Him. I desperately wanted to have an experience similar to the ones I had heard about. The one thing my young mind could not fathom was that I did not have to *try* so hard to have an encounter with Him. I could not earn His salvation. I just needed to believe in Jesus with all my heart, and He would give me my desires. I also did not yet understand the personal nature of how God would allow me to come to know Him.

These were my stumbling blocks until a wise evangelist led me along the road to faith in a short conversation. Her major question to me was simple: "Do you believe?" I am grateful for the mercy God showed me in my fearful state, for even as a little girl I needed His loving kindness.

Points to Ponder

1. What were the circumstances under which you realized you needed a Savior?
2. How did you know you had faith?

Chapter 3

Mercy Suits My Case

"I loved thee with an everlasting love, therefore with loving-kindness have I drawn thee."[1]

Like an inmate on death row, I sat waiting to die. I tried to improve myself as much as possible, hoping God would see me as worthy of entering the pearly gates of heaven. The harder I tried, the more difficult the task became. In the end, knowing that my righteousness was worse than the nastiest thing I could possibly imagine, I gave up and asked God to help me. That's when I came to see that He loved me just as I was.[2]

A Father's Love

It is difficult to place the chapters of this section in an appropriate order for such intimate work as God's intervention in our lives. The order here may imply that realization comes before mercy. This is not so, for God was at work long before we realized we needed Him.

An earthly father teaches his child from birth to do well, but he must let go when the child grows up. Similarly, God appears to let go when we rebel and push against His love. Yet He is watching lovingly as we stumble, waiting for the "aha!" moment to occur for us. His watching is not passive. He provides direction along the way.[3]

This fact has been a subject of debate for many people. Some feel that God meddles in human affairs too much and we are like puppets on a string being manipulated by the Almighty. Others believe He is too aloof to concern Himself with the daily, mundane antics of human beings, thus His eye is on the "big things" like nature. Still others are uncertain of the very existence of God, preferring to believe that people somehow evolved from some lower form of animal and that evolution will eventually improve upon what we now see as superior in human beings.

The Bible gives us some idea of the nature of God. It describes Him as having created us with intelligence and the ability to choose.[4] However, the fact that we have a choice does not mean we will not have to live with the consequences of our choices, whether positive or negative.

Relinquishing Control

When we freely admit our inability to control every aspect of our lives, what God does is nothing short of miraculous. Rather than entering into our lives to make us weak, He comes into us and lives through us. Thus, we find ourselves able to realize that "I can do all things through Christ, who strengthens me."[5]

We may accomplish great feats, and people may praise us for being great, but we know that if it weren't for Him, no one would see this greatness. Therefore, we humbly thank God for making us who we are. What the world does not understand is that we are not only humble, but we are *humbled* by the awesome power of God that is at work in us, helping us to stand in difficult times, giving us victory in the midst of defeat. That God allows Himself to work in such beings to accomplish His purpose is beyond our ability to fathom. The only term that explains it is *mercy*.

When we stumble, we usually try to find solutions to our problems. Sometimes we talk to others about our issues, but family members, friends, counselors, or coworkers all have one thing in common. Despite how well intentioned they may be, they are all human beings with their own frailties. They are much more shortsighted than the Almighty. Yet, because they are in front of us and they can show verbal and facial features and statements of approval or disapproval, we lean heavily on them.

Sometimes they are correct in their assessments of our situations, and sometimes they are not. Eventually we recognize they can't see into our problems like our heavenly Father can. When our support system lets us down, we understand we are seeking the wrong things from them. When they are no longer able to empathize with us we realize that people are just people. They can't provide what a soul requires.

We Need God

We need more than a quick answer for our latest problems, and that is what God is letting us discover: *We need Him.* When we are finished depending upon everyone else for validation, God is waiting to tell us of our true worth to Him. When we listen to Him, our restlessness fades and we are able to lead others to the Master. His mercy extends to those around us. We come to realize that no matter is too complicated, no issue too hopeless, no problem too great. Our lives are in His hands. And just as Jesus commended His spirit into the hands of the Father,[6] the one place we can be at total rest is in His hands.

Mercy does not end when we enter into intimacy with God through His dear Son. It is only the beginning, for many an experience awaits us after we begin to walk with Jesus. The enemy makes countless attempts to distract us from the purpose for which we have been born again.

Although there was a war to deter us from coming into the kingdom of God, further dangers await us during the process of growing into all that the Father intended. But praise God for His vigilance toward us. Praise Him for His mercy.

Points to Ponder

1. Upon whom or what have you leaned too heavily?
2. What events caused you to realize that your life was bigger than what people assumed?
3. When did you realize you needed God?

Part I – Conclusion

In a world that is trying hard to convince people of the invincible nature of man, it is refreshing to know that God is merciful and He knows our vulnerable state. Our minds, bodies, and spirits are subject to the same distractions that were offered to man at the beginning of time. The same force is at work today to convince us that we can become equal to God if we follow our own designated path, doing what God told us not to do.

No matter what the world is attempting to do, our heavenly Father is constantly calling us into a relationship with Him. He calls us through our love of nature, our relationships with those we love, the melodious music of a church organ. He calls us in the stillness of the night, in the sadness of our journeys, and in our moments of greatest despair. In times when nothing makes sense, when we've reached the end of our resources to help ourselves, when our inner ache cannot receive solace from anyone or anywhere else, He beckons. Even in our stubbornness to accept His help, He is calling our hearts through His mercy.

May we come to understand the depth to which our Father will go to draw us to Him from the darkness. May we lift Jesus up that He may draw others to the Father. Amen.

PART II

Now in the Light

Part II – Introduction

Angelica had always thought she was just like everyone else. She laughed at funny jokes, empathized with those who were hurting, and conducted herself as she had been taught from childhood. However, there came a time when she realized she was different. She was the one approached by people in her family and on her job when they were in desperate situations and wanted someone to pray for them. While she did not wear the outer trappings worn by some Christian women, such as long dresses, the light of Jesus shone as evidence of her faith.

Two women came to her and asked if she would lead them in a small group for Christian women who were married to men who were not believers. Their husbands were antagonistic toward Christianity, and they were feeling the pain.

Angelica's first response was that she was not a therapist and could not give advice on what should be done in their marriages. They said they were not looking for counseling, but they believed she understood the issues they were confronting. They just wanted Angelica to spend time with them. One said she had stayed in her marriage as long as she had only because she was watching Angelica.

This relationship grew into a strong Christian support system that lasted through the death of one husband and the departure of another. It drew other women who were refreshed by the conversation, food, and support. They were able to go home and love their husbands after each session.

How do we become so transparent that what occurs in our lives, whether successes or troubles, illustrates the love of Christ? You don't have to tell everyone about all that you're confronting. This isn't about telling all of our business to the world or smiling in the midst of pain so that others will think we have it all together. You don't stop having problems when you come to the Lord. Author Brennan Manning[1] says our suffering should not be hidden behind a fake smile in an effort to deceive the world with the thought that the Christian life is always pleasant. It is about being real in every situation. This is more endearing to our heavenly Father and to the world than a performance.

People discover that Jesus walks with us through the storms rather than taking us out of every situation. He teaches us to grow and develop into the mature people of faith we are meant to be. Because of our struggles, we are able to love others more deeply, to feel their pain. As Jesus experienced suffering and "was in all points touched with the feeling of our infirmity,"[2] so are we called to deeply love others and to intercede to the Father on their behalf. Our life struggles lead people to the Lord because He sent His Spirit to help us through our difficulties, and people can see what God is doing in us. Transparency in the light of God's goodness keeps us real, reminding us that our very existence depends on our Father.

The two discourses that follow describe the changes that occur in the lives of Christians as a result of being in Christ. These transformations mark a clearness that is obvious to the non-Christian as well as to the Christian, profoundly affecting our walk with Christ.

Chapter 4

Now We Are Light

I came to You, hungrier than I had ever been
    physically,
Knowing that if You did not fill me,
    I would die.
And when I took that first sip, and started
    becoming open to You,
I came to know I was at home in You.

No more trying to come out of my skin
To become someone else's version of
    who I am.
No more trying to make myself happy
By pleasing others and hoping they would
    approve.
I am a new creation, blood-bought, stripe-
    healed, and delivered!
I am becoming like You, Jesus, and I love
    what I see![1]

As a newborn Christian, Dee came to realize she did not want the same things she had before. She told her mate that she could not live with him any longer unless they were married. She brought her mom, sisters, and nieces to church in the hopes that they, too, would personally experience God. Each of them has accepted Christ and is still serving in the church. Until this day she remains tenderly aware of the changes God made in her life in terms of lifestyle, visions of herself in ministry, and her ability to go through difficult life situations and still remain full of faith in God.

Manny had had a long-time drug habit and had been clean for approximately one year when it occurred to him that he needed a relationship with the "higher power" referred to in his support group meetings. He came under deep conviction one Sunday morning during the worship and went to the front of the church at the invitation to receive Christ as Savior. In the ensuing weeks he attended a new believers' class, where he asked questions and learned what the Bible said about him. While no one told him to change his lifestyle, it became apparent that it was changing. The yellow stains on his teeth and the labored breathing dissipated because he no longer needed to smoke cigarettes. The manner in which he spoke to people and his later response to God's call to ministry further showed his deep concern for others like him who needed the Lord.

What happened to Dee and Manny and the rest of us gives evidence of the presence of the Holy Spirit in our lives once we accept Him as Savior. He will come down to our level to teach us what we need to know. He knows our capacity for understanding and how much we need Him to intervene. And He helps us to walk in His light so we can move to even greater intimacy with Him.

As Paul described to the church at Ephesus the ignorance, burden, and cloak under which we once lived, he said that we are no longer in darkness when we come to Christ, but are "light in the Lord."[2] This change is expressed as spiritual hunger and results in adjustments to the way we think about ourselves, those in our immediate surroundings, and the world at large. It also results in our daily spiritual renewal.

Hunger

When we first came to the knowledge of Christ as our Savior, our joy was unbounded and the freedom from guilt was unparalleled. We were like newborn babies, wanting to know everything about our Savior and how we should live for Him.[3]

Just as a baby must eat in order to grow into the person he/she will someday become, so the newly converted Christian "hungers and thirsts for righteousness."[4] This hunger is not only for spiritual food through the preached and taught Word of God, but also for fellowship with other believers who confirm and affirm him and model some of what God wants in His children. God, being the good Father that He is, would not give His child a "stone if he asked for bread, or a serpent if he asked for fish."[5] God is willing to give us "exceeding, abundantly, above all that we ask or think, according to the power that works in us."[6] Thus, He continually helps us to grow.

As a baby needs interaction with his mother in order to develop thinking and social skills, so the new Christian needs a personal relationship with the Father in order to develop into a mature Christian. Just as the mother calls the child's name and talks to him, so God calls the name of the new Christian and communes with him through fellowship in the church and in the spirit of the believer. Over time, this communion with God adds definition to the Christian, giving him courage, teaching him to trust in God, and telling him who he is in Christ.

Thoughts of Ourselves

Children of the light learn to walk soberly in faith and love, "having on the helmet of salvation."[7] As we become more equipped, the knowledge of who we are in Christ becomes clearer.

Each of us must answer the question of who we are in a personal way. The Scriptures that lead us to claim I am "the righteousness of Christ,"[8] I am "the head and not the tail,"[9] I am "the apple of God's eye,"[10] and so on, may bring temporary expressions of joy, but the reality of who we say we are is lived out in our lives every day. Not Just quote it

We tend to memorize Scriptures that build us up and allow others to fall upon deaf ears. When we are told we are immature Christians, we may plead temporary hearing or memory loss. However, God is telling us this for our own good. It may hurt our pride to see that we still need to grow, but He will indeed help us grow if we pay attention to Christ. We need to mature to be able to stand.

The Word of God directs our dealings with others and our treatment of ourselves. It will either enable us to step out and do what we are called to do by virtue of our knowledge of ourselves in Christ, or it will make us go to Him with a convicted heart because of our lack of knowledge. Self-knowledge is so important that throughout the New Testament and in instances of the Old Testament, there were constant reminders of who people were, both as a nation and individually. This was said in order to instill confidence in the people of their distinctive nature, which was evident in their thoughts about themselves and their conduct toward others.

One example is the greeting of Gideon by the angel who proclaimed, "Hail, mighty man of valor."[11] Because Gideon believed the angel had the wrong person, his response was lackluster. He came from the smallest Israelite family and was the lowest in his clan, so he did not believe he had any ability to save Israel from the treachery of the Midianites. The visit from the angel did not convince him of his destiny until after several signs were confirmed.

In Bible times, when children were born, they often received names associated with the circumstances of their birth. At times, an event during the pregnancy labeled the child. Coming out of his mother's womb, Jacob caught the heel of his twin brother, Esau, who was born first. Thus, he was named Jacob, meaning "supplanter," a name he lived to fulfill before becoming Israel, "the prince of God."[12]

Sometimes names were chosen due to prophecy about the child to be born. In some instances, the Lord God provided the name. Joseph was told to name Mary's first-born son Jesus, "because He shall save His people from their sins."[13]

Sometimes children were named due to parental attitudes. Sarah, at age one hundred, laughed when three heavenly men came to visit her husband, Abraham, and told him she would bear a son within a year's time. Thus, when the child was born, he was named Isaac, which meant "laughter."[14]

Some children are named as God directs. For instance, due to his unbelief in the prophecy of the angel about his son's impending birth, Zacharias was made mute until John the Baptist's birth. His tongue was released only after he gave his son the name John in obedience, as the angel of the Lord had said.[15]

In biblical times, the name signified who the child was, and he was expected to live out his name. However, sometimes the Father changed the name of a person when he or she was expected to live out God's higher purpose. Such was the case of Abram, Sarai, Jacob, and the New Testament Saul.

Today as in the past, God can change our thoughts and beliefs about our identity and our destiny, and we can be used for His purposes. Even though we are named by our earthly parents and given direct and subtle messages by others in our surroundings as to what is expected of us, God can help us see ourselves from His perspective. We can live out our names given to us by the Father.

54

Thoughts of Others in our Surroundings

What we think about ourselves in relationship to others will come out in the light of Christ. We will have to repent our shortsightedness before our holy God if we want to grow in intimacy with Him. As we develop in the knowledge of Christ, we become increasingly aware that our lives are an open book. We are living epistles. We have nothing to hide, nor are we able to hide any sin, shortcoming, or blemish from the light of Christ.

Scripture speaks of our daily inward renewal.[16] This takes place as a necessary outgrowth of our relationship with Christ and may happen without our awareness of the changes. Only after time has gone by do we notice our appetite for the base and secular has waned. This confirms in us that the Spirit of God has come to reside in us, and we are no longer our own, for we are "bought with a price."[17] "Our bodies are the temples of the Holy Spirit."[18]

As we move toward maturity in Christ, we may notice that the Holy Spirit is bringing about conviction in areas of our lives that we never even knew. As we stand as the light of the world, the light of Christ, we need to surrender our thoughts, feelings, and actions to Him. The sooner we pray to the Father about releasing these issues, the less apt we are to want to justify them, and the less likely they are to take root in our minds and affect our spiritual walk.

For example, each time Susan is in my presence, I feel insecure and angry. I may draw the conclusion that Susan is putting on airs, trying to make sure everyone knows what she has or how close she is to God.

However, Susan may not be doing anything like this. What has me rattled may be purely my own perception of her and my own insecurity about trusting God for everything in my life. Many times people come into our lives so that our own bitterness and insecurity may be excised from us, that our communion with the Father may be more free and clear. It is important to ask the Father about the feelings we are having and to be ready to release them as He reveals to us what is really going on in our hearts.

During Peter's short work with the Gentiles, God had told him in a vision to eat the meat of every four-footed beast he saw on a great sheet that was lowered into his presence.[19] Peter's response was that he would not eat the unclean animals. God ordered that Peter not call unclean what God had cleansed. God repeated His command, and Peter repeated his rebuttal. As Peter sat pondering the vision, the servant of a Gentile named Cornelius came to his door and requested that he come to the home of Cornelius to speak the things of the Lord. When Peter went there and heard Cornelius's concerns about the things of the Lord, he shared with him the gospel of Jesus Christ. As he spoke, the Holy Spirit fell on Cornelius and those in his household. These Gentile believers spoke in other languages, just as the Jewish followers of Christ had on the day of Pentecost. Peter's perception of God changed. He acknowledged that He "does not show favoritism,"[20] that He would bring believing Gentiles into intimacy with Him as He had done with the Jewish disciples.

However, even after he saw the works of God on them, Peter still had reservations about having fellowship with Gentiles. When his fellow Jews came to greet the brethren, Peter separated himself from the Gentiles. He feared that he would be not deemed a strict observer of Jewish law. Later, in Peter's writing, we see evidence of a clearer understanding of the grace of God and an allusion to God's work of salvation among the Gentiles.[21]

Thoughts of the World

Some parts of our lives are to be seen by the world. The way in which we understand our vulnerabilities and improve upon our shortcomings and pains can be a blessing to the world.[22]

Just as Paul and Silas sat in jail after speaking out in the name of the Lord Jesus Christ,[23] we are sometimes treated harshly for righteousness' sake and must bear some pain.[24] In their case, they had been beaten and were awaiting whatever further punishment their captors would levy upon them. We do not know what their conversation or actions consisted of before midnight.

Perhaps they tried to dab the wounds they had suffered or encouraged each other not to lose hope. Maybe they planned their strategy for their next encounter with the magistrates. Whatever the conversations earlier, at midnight God gave them hearts of praise and adoration to Him in the presence of their fellow prisoners. He sent an angel to release the bands of all the prisoners.

The Lord God turned the tables and put the jailor at His mercy. This man considered ending his life in fear of his impending torture for being irresponsible toward the prisoners. But the jailor heard the confident voices of the apostles telling him they were yet in the jail, having no reason to escape.[25] Rather than turning His wrath upon the jailor, God chose to deliver him from a state of bondage far greater than that of his captives.

Having come into the light of Christ, the jailor found himself lacking and asked for direction in order to be saved. He received the Word of God, and his life was now in the hands of the Lord Jesus Christ.

One of his first acts following his conversion and the baptism of everyone in his household was to wash the wounds of the men of God and feed them. Is this not how the Lord handles our burdens today? In the midst of binding situations in which the enemy seeks to crush us because of our faith, He gives us peace that rings out a song in the night. Others are brought to the light of Christ in the midst of our trials. In leading them to Christ, we are set free.

Every experience of the Christian is an opportunity for someone to see Christ in our lives. The most important thing the Christian can do to leave an impact on the world is to live. Live so the world can see Christ at work in you.

Daily Renewal

Today, rather than changing our own names, we are given the name of Christ through spiritual rebirth. Much like the days of old, we are expected to live out this name. As children of the light, transformation is expected to take place as we become more like Christ each day.

✦ However, this transformation is not contrived. It is humanly impossible for us to maintain ourselves in a transformed state outside of the work of the Holy Spirit. The transformation is not so much outward at first, but we experience small rebirths in our thought life and communion with the Father.[26]

✦ The Scripture that describes our new walk with Christ should be read carefully and prayerfully. "Therefore if any man be in Christ he is a new creature, old things are passed away and behold all things are become new."[27] This passage speaks of our newness as spiritual beings in Christ. As a result, we live life for the One who died for us and know one another from a spiritual viewpoint, not strictly by human standards.[28]

This transformation is gradual, with fits and starts. We receive messages from all around us. Some of those messages are not appropriate for who we are. At other times, the treatment we receive is beneath us, and it may bring us down if we accept what people say about us. As we deal with people throughout our days, being battered by life's trials, temptations, and tribulations, our best hope is to look to the Master daily and seek the answer to the question, "Lord, who do you say I am?" As we grapple with this new knowledge of one another and ourselves, may we know Christ to a greater depth than ever fathomable.

Points to Ponder

1. What new or different ways of thinking assured you that you were indeed a Christian?

2. How has your life's walk changed since you became a Christian?

Chapter 5

The Place of "Becoming"

Through the Lord's mercies we are not consumed, because His compassions fail not. They are new every morning: great is Thy faithfulness.[1]

After the disciples had followed Jesus for three years and were convinced of His divinity and purpose, Jesus said to Peter, "Simon, Simon, Satan has desired to have you that he may sift you as wheat, but I have prayed for you that your faith fail not."[2] Just as He warned Peter, as the people of God, we are called to give our all to the Master. We are also to be watchful, but not to give over to fear. The fact that Jesus prayed for Peter reassures us that the result is our ability to be abundantly victorious because of His love for us.[3]

More than a Clean Life

After we have followed Christ for some time, at times we tend to become complacent, feeling that we have passed the most difficult tests of our lives with God. After all, those temptations to lie when it was convenient or to indulge in other vices have been conquered in our Christian walk. We can be lulled to sleep, thinking that all there is to the Christian walk is living a clean life. However, even the most seasoned of Christians may inadvertently allow our walk to become our idol. I know some Christians who are quick to declare that they never drunk alcoholic beverages or engaged in promiscuous lifestyles. They wear this information as if it were a badge of honor. Some, having been rescued by God from a life of sin, hold up their clean lives as trophies for the world to see. This may make some people want what we have, but more often than not, such boasting makes others feel unworthy and alienated from what these people have achieved.

Sometimes when we witness to people, we point to how God cleaned up our lives as evidence of the change He can make in their lives. But the change of lifestyle is an indication of a much deeper victory. The victory achieved is not so much our changed lives, although righteousness and clean living are important to God.

Some unbelievers get cleaned up on special programs. Others, through self-discipline, are victorious over vices in their lives. Thus we cannot assume the Christian life is only about clean living.

Giving one's life to Jesus is not simply one of many options to explore to get free of drugs, alcohol, sexual addictions, or other undesirable ways. The victory, rather than our righteousness, is our faith in Jesus.[4] According to John, the ones who are "born of God have overcome the world." In verse five he says, "Who is he that overcomes the world, but he that believes that Jesus is the Son of God."[5] The writer to the Hebrews said, "Without faith it is impossible to please God, for he that comes to God must believe that He is, and that He is a rewarder of those who diligently seek Him."[6]

Purpose through Faith

one word what does it mean 1st natural → then Spirit

Throughout Jesus' walk on earth, He constantly encouraged His disciples to believe in Him.[7] He reminded them that with man the works He did were impossible, but that everything was possible with God.[8] He asked His disciples on one occasion who they believed He was.[9] In this question lies the crux of His mission: to convince the world of His divinity and to fulfill the mission set forth by His Father, redeeming us to the Father through faith in Him.

The answer to the question of purpose is easily stated but not easily lived, for there are many noble causes to which one may be joined. What is most important is that we have faith in God in the name of His Son, Jesus.

Just as Jesus followed His Father's purpose on earth, we are to walk likewise. It is glorious to have an understanding of the purpose for which you were saved. Such a realization brings new meaning to every activity in which you are engaged. Your life is now centered on the purpose for which you were brought into the kingdom of God. Replenishment in worship is enacted in order for you to go out and be who you are called to be, from which comes the ability to do what you are called to do. Confidence that one is accomplishing God's will exudes the Christian who moves purposefully throughout the day. The desires to continue to do God's will, despite severe opposition, come from knowing that you are fulfilling the purpose for which you were called. This holy inner drive takes you to the realization that the end of this accomplishment in life may be physical death, yet you will continue in life eternal.

This place of becoming requires having faith in God in the midst of uncertainty about the next step or when we will reach the ultimate destination. Some of us want to do God's will so badly that we get caught up in the deeds and forget the One who called us. I believe God sometimes makes us wait because He knows we are not ready. The work is so important, He wants to build godly character into our lives that will keep us in His path. Is this not a loving deed the Father enacts? He does not want us to suffer or become impatient waiting on our ministry. He does not want us to make up something just to get started. He wants us to become what He has called us to be and to understand that what we *do* can never replace who we are *becoming*. When He said through Paul to Timothy, "Do the work of an evangelist,"[10] He wanted him to maintain who he was in Christ while doing a specific work.

Yielding to His Prompts

All of this discussion regarding the journey has to do with surrender. Our presupposition regarding what is ahead, how it will be, and what people will think must be handed over to the Master. Otherwise, they become distractions put in front of us to make a shipwreck of our lives.

I once made a funny but frightening observation. I was watching a relative learn to drive. She became so enamored with the way she looked while driving that she took her eyes off the road and began watching us, saying, "Look, I'm driving!" Had she not had a good teacher, she could surely have had a wreck that day. However, her teacher quickly said, "Watch the road," bringing her attention back to the business of driving. Is not this the way it is with us? We get caught up in the deed and how we will look doing it. We worry more about the reactions of the ones being served than the One we are serving. But praise be to God who loves us, we have an excellent Teacher who brings our attention back to the Father. Jesus sent the Holy Spirit to guide us and teach us all things.

Points to Ponder

1. In what charitable acts do you engage?
2. In what ways does your Christian walk motivate you to greater intimacy with Christ?
3. What acknowledgments in life have distracted you from your real purpose?

4. Are you yet released from the distractions?

acknowledging,
and working on it

Part II – Conclusion

It takes experience walking in the light of Christ to understand that the Christian life is not like any other. We do not contrive the changes that occur in our lives as the way in which we should conduct ourselves. Instead, the Christian life of identification with Christ changes our thinking about God's work in the world and who we are in Christ. This identification is not merely a mental exercise, but a spiritual experience in which we are lived through. This is why Jesus said His "yoke is easy."[1] Our greatest efforts alone amount to failure, but when we allow the Spirit of God to live through us, everything changes. We view our families, coworkers, and friends differently when we look through the eyes of the Master. The Holy Spirit engineers the walk. In order to live in the light, we must live a life of surrender.

PART III

Surrender

"Far from being a sign of weakness, only surrender to something or someone bigger than us is sufficiently strong to free us from the prison of our egocentricity. Only surrender is powerful enough to overcome our isolation and alienation."

— David Benner,
from *Surrender to Love*
(Downers Grove, IL:
InterVarsity Press, 2003), 10

Part III – Introduction

J ust watch daytime soap operas, talk shows, reality television programs, and movies to understand what keeps some of us from seeing the benefits of a life surrendered to Christ. Some of it is fear that the One to whom we surrender cannot be trusted. Many of us have had experiences in which we gave ourselves to someone not worthy of trust and were deeply damaged. For some people the fear has seethed in their souls for so long that it has solidified into anger. Believing themselves strong, they have become crusaders for other vulnerable people, unable and unwilling to forgive.

For others, hopelessness pervades their lives. If it is not arrested, suicide—whether slow and painless or quick and horrific—will be their lot. Whether as a result of a choice in life or an illness, events can render us unable to reach out to others, even those worthy of trust.

Two women in the Bible had horrific experiences that could have left them feeling all of the above emotions at different points in their lives.

However, each of them reached a defining moment when only the choice of Jesus was appropriate and she had to reach out in faith to Him. The woman with the alabaster box[1] and the woman with the issue of blood[2] were outcasts from society. They had every reason to distrust anyone who reached out to them. They had cause to be angry because of their situations and to lose hope of ever being accepted. However, both of these women decided to publicly reach out to Jesus. Abandoning any thoughts or aspirations of preserving their pride, they approached the Master in total surrender.

Following an examination of the possible internal struggles experienced by each of these women, we will continue our discussion about the One to whom they surrendered. We will end with a discourse on the meaning of surrendering to Christ. Each of us, in order to walk more closely with Christ, will have to come to this point in our lives. Whether as a result of comfort or discomfort, illness or health, we will all have to decide whether it is worth it to surrender.

Chapter 6

The Boldness of Surrender

When I am finally fully enraptured with
    your wonderful grace,
When my vision is only of your marvelous
    face,
Must I wait until then to give you my all?
Or can I come with some distractions,
    fighting all the way?

Will You take me, while I'm struggling to be
    brave?
Can You take my insecurities, fears, and low
    self-esteem, and still accept my praise?
I have nothing to hide, nor anything to offer
    that is not riddled with trouble.
Can You use me, Lord? Will You?[1]

The Master forgave Mary, a woman with a bad
reputation. Her heart overflowed with gratitude
for the Master's loving kindness. In her day, as it is

today, there were those who looked down on people who had made terrible choices in their lives. Their actions against such persons were exclusionary, condemning, and condescending. Their conversation about the sinner was halfhearted pitying and sarcastic, denying any possibility that such a person could ever change.

Mary had encountered a man who was different from any other. Although He lived among them, He had a redemptive message. His perceptions of the motives of people were keen, penetrating, and one hundred percent accurate. He knew when someone was lying and putting on a show of piety. He knew if you'd risk what little dignity you had left to get to Him. And He'd receive you if you worshipped God in your spirit and in truth.

Maybe Mary anticipated that she would not be accepted—the wondering stares at what business *she* had being at Simon's house; the hopes of her detractors that the Master would reject her, particularly since she had probably not cleansed herself according to Levitical mandates. Little did they know this woman with such a burden of sin had been completely cleansed according to a heavenly order. Even if they couldn't see the difference in her, she knew beyond a shadow of doubt that she was not the same woman who once could not be satisfied by anything this life had to offer. This was not a change she could have brought about of her own volition, not in a million attempts. Her transformation had come from a power greater than her hurts, greater than her embarrassment, greater than her appetites. The difference in her could only be found in Jesus.

The Unlikely Anointer

Thus Mary went to Jesus, her source, and brought Him something that, unlike her, had not been broken, something that cost her much, something that, once opened, could never be returned to its container. She had been broken, and the pain of her brokenness had been excruciating. So she brought Him a symbol of her newly healed life: body, spirit, and soul. She opened herself for the world to see the Spirit that now lived in her. And oh, what a sweet aroma she emitted. No more rank with the odor of her infamous past, her worship was now holy and acceptable to God.

She broke the container and anointed Jesus, the One who baptized with the Holy Spirit. *She,* of all people, anointed *Him.* What a sight for all to see! Their disapproval meant nothing to her. She was in the presence of her Savior, the only man who looked at her without intentions of taking advantage of her. She had wondered if she could ever begin life again, and He had shown her the way. What a rapturous experience!

While Jesus supported her actions, others criticized her waste. Was He so arrogant that He would allow such extravagance to be poured out on Him? Did He not know the economic state of the poor in this place and time, and how many of them could have received assistance at the sale of this oil?

He knew well what the oil cost, even beyond the money. Does not God, the Son, deserve our very best?

Our most costly endeavors need to be totally broken and surrendered to Him without reservation. Does He not deserve our total attention and worship, despite the criticisms we may receive from others about our personal worth and value? What is the word of man worth next to the Word of God?

A Commendation

Jesus spoke to the onlookers regarding Mary's deed words that would bring silence to the people and a new understanding of the meaning of worship. He talked of the significance of the act as a preparation for His burial and said that it would not go unnoticed as a historical event. Even though she had no intentions of doing this for her own notoriety, she became famous in her humility. She teaches us much without uttering one word. Jesus promises the same commendation to us in heaven if we pursue Him, present our bodies for His use, and allow our faith in Him to endure until the end of our lives.

Priorities

This woman's story teaches us the humiliation involved in the act of surrender, particularly in today's society in which one has to win over others at all costs. It teaches us that connecting with God is more important than saving face and this relationship is worth enduring a degrading situation.

The value of pursuing God in the midst of shame calls to mind the touching account of Bernadette Soubirous,[2] a young peasant girl who later was beatified a saint in the Catholic church. This young girl, having seen visions of a lady, was enraptured in the presence of God on many occasions. During one of those times, as curious and devout townspeople looked on, she claimed to have been directed by the angel of the Lord to a fountain that no one else saw. Bernadette washed her face in what appeared to others as dirt. People who were watching thought she was a lunatic. As the days ensued after that spectacle, people noticed a small spring at first, which eventually increased in size. Many people came to this site over the years that followed and were healed of their diseases. Later, as was directed by the woman in the vision, a chapel was built there in honor of our Lord Jesus, which is still attended.

X The world would rather be entertained than see the reality of worship. People who desire only what is edifying to them don't want to see the opposite done, especially in service to an invisible God. Secular humanism promotes a self-centered philosophy: if it pleases me, then it is appropriate. If it does not suit me, it must be eliminated.

It is our nature to put ourselves first and to save ourselves when faced with the possibility of humiliation. But worship involves putting God first, whether or not one looks good during the experience. It is a process to get to the place where it matters not what people think, because your desire to be in communion with God outweighs everything else. *So profound! Lord help me*

Privacy Is Not Always Available

One does not always have a private place in which to surrender to the need to worship God. In many cases, worship is public, and it is not always attractive to human sensibilities. But giving our very best and most costly attributes has a sweet aroma to the Father and the Son. As ministers, the probability of having to surrender publicly is increased by the sheer number of times we are ministering before the congregation. Thus we are well advised to follow Him at all costs rather than worrying about public reputations and secular advancement.

Selflessness

The prayers of the martyred saints are compared to a bowl of incense.[3] These people gave themselves wholly to God and were tortured because of their faith. This is gruesome to the naked eye, but it is precious in God's sight. In this day and time and in various parts of the world, Christians are still being tortured for their faith. They are being told to either renounce their faith or face extreme pain or physical death. Others are given fewer benefits of citizenship because they are Christians. In either case, the relinquishment of self-interests for the sake of others seems to be a prerequisite for selflessness.

It Doesn't Always Make Sense

Surrender is not readily explainable to the logical mind. For a person to enter into communion as a blood-bought child of God, to offer God words of appreciation, and to allow Him to see selfless service done with full knowledge that it may meet with the disapproval of the world represents unparalleled boldness.

As we have seen from this woman's life, we must approach the Son deliberately and boldly with no regrets, no explanations, and no reservations. Considering the wonderful gift of life given to us and the undeserved mercy shown by a loving God, may we shower Him with the costly worship He deserves in the midst of circumstances, whether private or public. Amen.

Points to Ponder

1. What are you most grateful to God for that takes you out of yourself and into complete worship? *His love and care for me.*
2. Are you prepared to surrender yourself to Him in the midst of public scrutiny? *yes,*

Chapter 7

The Healing in Surrender

The woman with the issue of blood was somewhat different from the woman with the alabaster box in her approach to the Master. In her case it was not out of thanksgiving or worship that she pressed toward Him. She had been ill for a long time. Having spent all that she could, she went to see if Jesus could make her well.

Imagine what must have happened to this woman. After wondering for a long time what was wrong with her body, she finally discovered a doctor who had seen cases like hers before. What a relief to find out the diagnosis! Next she learned what to do in order to be cured. But rather than finding a lasting cure, she suffered one setback after another. One treatment she received did nothing, but another gave her hope. The symptoms subsided for a while, but the cause did not, and the symptoms returned. Once the condition started, she was powerless to end it. Many times a doctor's advice or a well-meaning neighbor gave her hope. But the seesaw effect was exasperating. At the end of her finances and with nowhere else to turn, she was ready to quit.

But what she was giving up was more than she could bear. According to Levitical law, a woman who was bleeding or any person who had an issue of bodily fluids was considered unclean.[1] This meant she could not go to the temple to worship. Others were not to touch her. Thus, to give up would be to stop her very existence. David said, "I was glad when they said unto me let us go into the house of the Lord,"[2] but she could no longer be glad when she was invited to the temple because she could not enter. She would have to be on the sidelines rather than in the thick of the women's group.

Given her physical limitations and the social implications that came about as a result, this woman could not be timid about having her needs met. She could not allow herself to sit in self-pity or to be drained of whatever drive she might have left. Once she heard about Jesus, she must have engaged in self-talk to strengthen her resolve to get to Him despite all opposition she might encounter.

What I Say to Me

The significance of self-talk is not to be under-rated. Despite all that people may try to say, the voice we hear first and believe most is our own. Every word from someone else is filtered through our thoughts. We incorporate into our self-talk whatever is consis-tent and discard everything else. The only time we change what we believe about ourselves is when we can no longer confirm our thoughts by circumstances or persons upon whom we rely for validation.

This is true in negative as well as positive self-talk situations. For example, if I think everyone is out to get me, no matter what people say to make me believe they are not, I will continue to believe it. When I meet someone who helps me repeatedly without asking for anything in return, I am suspicious that he will eventually want something that will be devastating to me. If the time never comes when he demands anything of me, I may change my view about that person by saying, "Everyone except this person is out to get me."

It takes time to abandon one's own self-talk. It also takes Someone greater than a mind, Someone more powerful, Someone who can make a mind see the ineffable.

This woman with the issue, having suffered for many years, spoke a message of hope to herself. She had no more money to pay a doctor, and she must have been at the end of her wits trying to get well. She had no choice but to speak in positive terms to herself.

As she went into the street to get to Jesus, she most likely realized it would be more difficult than she had originally thought. At this point, the only thing standing between her and a healing was a large crowd of people and herself. Looking at the crowd, she could easily have given up. After all, she could not have been very strong, having been ill for twelve years. Watching for a break in the crowd probably would have been a good strategy. However, watching for Jesus was even better. When He got close to where she was standing she should jump in and let the crowd carry her, right? But how far would they take her? If she did not reach Him, would she be able to get out of the crowd and walk back home? No, the stakes were too high for a passive jump into a moving crowd. She needed to be deliberate. She needed to be aggressive. "The kingdom of heaven suffers violence and *the violent take it by force!*"[3] Jesus had said. Thus, she began self-talk. "*If I could but touch the hem of His garment I will be made whole.*"[4]

The Power of a Hem

In the Old Testament, the hem was a fringe on the mantle or cloak, placed as a reminder of God's commandments.[5] This went beyond the typical memorial experience. It was also a roadmap to God. The word from the Lord was to "remember, and do all my Commandments, and be holy unto your God."[6] He guaranteed them that other nations would take them by the hem to follow them to God.

What a powerful promise! In the woman's day Jesus, the Word incarnate, the Commandment of God in the flesh, dwelt among men, and wore on His garment the very symbol that would point others to His heavenly Father. No wonder the woman went for His hem! In touching the hem, she knew she would be made whole. While everyone else went after the man whom she was physically unable to reach, she went after His essence.

Jesus' reaction made total sense. According to Mark's account, he said, "Who touched my clothes?"

Luke says that Jesus said, "Who touched me?" Each of these authors described what happened.[7] To the natural eye, all that the woman did was touch His clothes, but we know she did much more. She touched the commandment of God. She touched Jesus with her faith.

New Paradigms

Many times we hang on to the way in which we have always thought about things or the pattern set by those we admire. But what if Jesus were passing by, and like this woman, we had to surrender all of the ways in which we thought things ought to be done in order to get to Him? What if, when He came by, we had no more to give and no other choice but to throw ourselves at His garment? Would we release our ways in order to touch Him? The Father said, "As high as the heavens are from the earth, that is how far My ways are from your ways, and My thoughts from your thoughts."[8]

A wise woman once said to me, "Sometimes we take ourselves too seriously." She meant we don't always understand everything, nor are we able to provide an answer to every question we have. But God knows, and He understands. If we stick with Him and trust Him wholly, we don't have to worry.

This wise woman is my mother, who at the age of sixty-nine suffered a damaging stroke after heart bypass surgery. After having been an active woman who raised seven children and supported her husband in ministry, I sometimes wonder how she continues to look up. She is no longer able to travel long distances without extraordinary plans being made for her care. She still sings praises to God with an impaired voice in her home and sometimes sheds tears of praise during church services. In her own way, my mother is pressing into Jesus, worshipping even in her debilitated state and receiving His gracious love. Just as the woman with the issue touched Jesus, my mother is touching His very essence. Her surrender helps her caretakers look to God, talk about God, and yearn for God. Through her sickness, God is drawing people to Him.

Even in our lack of understanding, Jesus makes the difference to a dying and hurting world. May we bask in the revelation of God's truth as we move into greater intimacy with Him.

Points to Ponder

1. What do you need to surrender in order to press into God's miraculous presence?
2. Are you willing to continue to press even when you don't see the desired result?

Chapter 8

Surrender to Whom?

In order to even consider surrendering, a person must believe that the opponent he or she faces is formidable and insurmountable. Any view of the weakness of the opponent or a strong view of one's own might keeps the person fighting to keep his independence, believing that he can win the battle. But what if we are not even aware of the identity of our enemy?

Saul, prior to being named Paul, was not aware at first that He was fighting against God. He thought he was operating on God's side and doing His will as he attempted to rid the world of the Christians. He was zealous, "an Hebrew of Hebrews, touching the law, blameless."[1] Yet there was a nagging at his inward self that he might be mistaken. God was knocking on his heart, yet because of the way he had always thought, he ignored Him for quite a while. "I am Jesus Whom you are persecuting. It is hard for you to kick against the pricks."[2] Saul discovered that the very God whose law he claimed to love was the One against whom he had waged war.

An Intelligent Choice

The defining moment in a conflict is when a person discovers the person against whom they are fighting. After such discovery one must carefully consider the choices in order to survive: fight, flight, or surrender. Saul realized that the One against whom he was fighting was the God of Abraham, Isaac, and Jacob. He had to have remembered the stories of deliverance of old, how no army was a match against God's people as long as God was fighting for them. He must have remembered the law, the perfection in it and its intent to admonish man to be single-minded toward God. The commandment "You shall have no other gods before Me"[3] had to have rung true in his mind and heart. "I am the Lord, that is my name, and my glory will I not give to another"[4] had to have made Him want to destroy these people who, he believed, were robbing God. Yet on the road to Damascus, as he was about to persecute more Christians, this Man spoke to him, knocking him from his horse.

Saul could not fight Him. His physical condition, which now mirrored his spiritual state, disoriented him. He was unable to flee from the presence of his enemy, for he was blinded and his horse was no longer under his control. Unable to fight or flee, it was time for Saul to surrender, for Saul was no match against God. His opponent apprehended and completely disabled him.

Many people have not taken a good look at their opponent and have not given their lives to Christ. We can be utterly lost if we are not diligent about surrendering our bodies, minds, and wills to God. We can be like Saul, doing "God's will," yet so far off the path that we are in danger of hurting the people who belong to the God we claim to love, of working against rather than for the kingdom of God.

Jesus said, "Not everyone that says to me 'Lord, Lord' will enter into the kingdom of heaven?"[5] He also spoke of those who try to reason their way in. "Have we not prophesied in your name? And in your name have cast out devils? And in your name done many wonderful works?" The damning statements that follow show that Christ's main concern is not with our works, but with whether we know Him. "I never knew you: depart from me, ye that work iniquity." This proclamation condemns us to depart from His wonderful presence if we make the main thing in our lives the work we do rather than a relationship with the One by whom we are known. We are not worthy opponents against God. He knows our secret thoughts and intentions, and He wants more than anything to have a relationship with us. In the midst of our messy lives, God loves us. He will help us with the mess, but we must trust Him.

Empty Works

Many who have not made sure of their walk with Christ have begun a *work* without a *relationship*. "Make your calling and election sure"[6] so that in the day when you stand before God, your name will be found written in the Lamb's book of life.

But what of those of us who *are* sure of our salvation? Many of us can still remember the day when we came to know Jesus as our Savior, but are tired from the long road we are traveling. We may remember the joy we had when we first believed. However, somewhere along the way, we became more concerned with the work and less concerned with the One who assigned us the work.

Does this happen to those of us who are genuinely born again? The apostle Paul reminded the Galatians, who began with Christ, "You did run well. Who has bewitched you?"[7] The church at Galatia had fervent faith in Jesus and became confused with the faith-works debate. They had received the Spirit of God and then lost their momentum because someone taught that they needed to do other things in order to please God. They were told they had to be circumcised in order to be pleasing to God.

Paul wrote to them in a tone of disappointment, but like the teacher he was, he helped them understand the grace of God. He described his experience of coming to Christ and how he was taught by revelation of God, not by men. He told them of the time when he met with the apostle Peter and they discussed the ministry to which Paul was called and had been working. They agreed that each had been called to bring Christ to a different group of people: Peter to the Jews, who continued to practice circumcision, and Paul to the Gentiles, who never had nor needed to begin such a practice.

The Jerusalem council of apostles agreed that the legalistic responsibilities placed upon the Jews would not be required of the Gentiles. However, Peter's communion with the Gentile Christians when no other Jewish Christians were there and his sudden separation from them at the arrival of more Jews magnified the differences. Paul spoke out against the hypocrisy of such an act and discussed at length the justification by faith that is not possible by works. He concluded that anything else in favor of justification by law was tantamount to a [frustration of] "the grace of God: for if righteousness come by the law, then Christ is dead in vain."[8] This statement is not to be taken lightly, for our faith rests upon the death, burial, and resurrection of Christ.

If it were possible to be justified by the works required by the law, there would be no need for the death of Jesus Christ. However, rather than leave us to wonder about its worth, Paul says the law came after God made the covenant with Abraham. The law came to reveal to us our guilt so that we could receive the grace of God. This tells us of the importance of receiving Christ by faith. God is not comparing our lives to the laws of the Old Testament, counting us as known or unknown by Him just because we received or rejected His circumcision.

In Old Testament times, this bloody deed of circumcision was committed as an act of cleanliness and a symbol of the preeminence of God. When Paul spoke of circumcision, he referred to our circumcision as "of the heart" rather than of the flesh.[9] Some outward customs and traditions were instituted by

God to point us to His inward work. Yet they have become so ingrained in our practice that it is difficult to remember what they really mean. Thus we are rendered unable to fully comprehend the depth to which God will go to bring us into communion with Himself.

Learn to Discern

Isn't this the way it is for us as well? We live our lives the way we think God wants. Some Christian conduct is clearly spelled out in His Word. "Abstain from fornication,"[10] "Flee youthful lusts,"[11] "Resist the devil and he will flee from you,"[12] and other Scriptures plainly tell us to avoid or resist certain sins. However, in this age of grace, during which we see other things that were not in existence during biblical times, we must depend upon the Word of God in our hearts and the direction of the Holy Spirit to guide us.

We sometimes cannot discern the devil. The Scriptures say sometimes he disguises himself as an angel of light.[13] Yet in our zeal for the Lord, we hold practices over the heads of others, claiming them not to be Christians if they don't do things as we do. This may make us feel secure, but it does not make God happy. We need to take a hard look at ourselves in the light of God's loving grace. If we are honest, we will admit that God has been calling us to greater intimacy with Him to surrender our all. Yet, in our fear of intimacy and of trusting anyone outside our own experiences, we have pushed away rather than drawn closer to Him.

Many of us spend countless hours studying the Scriptures. But they must be prayerfully studied with full knowledge that God speaks to us through them and that Jesus is the embodiment of the Scriptures. Jesus said, "You search the Scriptures, for in them you think you have eternal life, but they testify of me."[14] Sometimes in our quest to be good, we miss the only One who is good.

When His disciples marveled and rejoiced at having demons subject to them, Jesus told them not to rejoice because of this, but because "your name is written in heaven."[15] Jesus told us we would do greater works than He because He was going to His Father.[16] Yet we must put works and faith into perspective. We are not to become so wrapped up in what we do that we forget the One who called us. Even our rejoicing in His work through us should be because of where our names are written, because we are known by Him.

When Jesus prayed for Lazarus in the presence of His disciples and the mourners, He had absolute concentration upon His Father. He acknowledged that He needed the Father to raise Lazarus.[17] This speaks volumes for us. We should not look upon the acts we are doing for the kingdom without also rejoicing over His relationship with us. God's works through us are marvelous, particularly because He loves us and will do them for us because of our intimate relationship with Him.

God Loves Us

This love of the Father, exemplified by His Son, Jesus, brings about the surrender. Although God has all power, He does not choose to show it to us in brawn, but rather in His enveloping, unfathomable love for us. We experience His love in the way He takes care of us daily despite our shortcomings, in the way He provides a way out of our struggles, and in the way He dwells with us in our unbearable moments. In the silence and the darkness referred to by St. John of the Cross,[18] as our trust in Him is allowed to grow, we become more confident in His love. In the way in which He picks us up from our worst falls and embraces us in our brokenness, we come to know how precious He finds us. May we continue to surrender to His loving prompts, allowing the Holy Spirit to give us grace to accept what we find impossible to do for ourselves. May we receive the love of God in every aspect of our lives, allowing His healing and worshipping at His feet. Amen.

Points to Ponder

1. What is your motivation for what you do as a Christian?
2. Are you aware of how deeply God loves you?

Chapter 9

The Meaning of Surrender

I beseech you therefore, brethren, by the
mercies of God, that ye present your bodies
a living sacrifice, holy, acceptable unto God,
which is your reasonable service. And be
not conformed to the world: but be ye transformed by the renewing of your mind, that ye
may prove what is that good, and acceptable,
and perfect, will of God.[1]

The act of surrender is like no other work in the
life of man. In our society we are taught from
our youth to be self-sufficient, "pulling ourselves up
by our own bootstraps." While we are supposed to
learn how to work in teams in almost every industry,
it is the strength of the individual that is most praised.
Surrender is not accepted as a dignified act, nor is it
given the praise one would expect to get if it were
indeed a prized attribute of human existence. Yet we
are begged by the apostle Paul in the above discourse

to surrender our bodies as our Lord Jesus Christ gave His. Rather than being asked to be sacrifices of atonement, or sin offerings, we are asked to be *living, vibrant,* and *fertile* sacrifices.

Most of us, when asked for the definition of a sacrifice, conjure up the vision of an offering that dies a horrific death in order to appease an angry god. However, Paul urges us to continuously present our bodies alive. He goes on to ask us to be changed by the renewing of our minds. The implication of this statement is that we are to live for Him in a sacrificial state. But what does that entail?

This is where the world usually stops listening to the church. Everyone has his or her view of living a life for God, and usually that means no enjoyment in life. We picture a woman wearing long dresses of drab colors, with no make-up or adornments. Her mind is heavenward, with no thought of how she is perceived by the world. Yet Jesus went to great lengths to tell us what our role is. He likened the church to salt and light.[2] He described salt as having taste, saying if the salt loses its taste it is good for nothing. What strong terms!

What is a salty church like? It invites individuals to be involved and accepted. Love flows among its members and to the world, making it simple to come to Jesus. The world becomes thirsty for Jesus because church members have a continuous, satisfying, intimate relationship with Jesus. It takes surrender to be the salt of the earth, for our selfish attitudes tell us to leave people alone, to stay aloof, and to keep people at arm's length. But our relationship with

Christ encourages us to share what we have with the world.

As the light of the world, we are on display for the world to see. We need not be surprised when the world makes a spectacle of a Christian leader who falls into temptation. As a "city set on a hill,"[3] the presence of Jesus in us gives the world a vision of Him. This is why it is so important for the church to be real, honest, and forgiving. When we hold up a lofty image of a Christian that we can't live up to, we are setting ourselves up for failure. The world needs to watch us go through triumphs as well as struggles, heartaches, disappointments, and grief. The manner in which we go through life testifies to the constant presence of the invisible, immutable, omnipotent God. The manner in which we treat our bodies and the way in which our thinking has changed as a result of spending time with the Lord distinguishes us from the world.

The Body

Paul divides the experience of surrender into two distinct parts: the body and the mind. This combination is important, particularly to people who are used to practicing spiritual things with the body only. For example, love is evident when people hug one another. Peace is described as closed eyes, and low, calming voice tones. The physical provides the evidence of the ineffable for the world to see.

To go beyond the visible and allow our identities to emanate from within is not easy. We have the God-given right of choice about our interior and exterior lives, and we may find ourselves changing our minds about presenting ourselves as sacrifices under difficult circumstances. Yes, giving up your physical body is difficult because you want to continue with what feels good, whether it is to remain comfortable or prevent pain. Yet we are called upon at times to commit ourselves to fasting—denying ourselves for a season of the delicacies that make life sweet—for a higher spiritual cause. We are called upon to comfort others rather than thinking first of ourselves. We are also called to worship God at times when we feel like withdrawing from everyone and everything, and just nursing our wounds. We are called upon to pray when we wish to retaliate, to illustrate our faith in the Scripture that tells us that vengeance is in God's hands.[4] We are called upon to believe the word of the Lord when our circumstances tell us to be practical and cut our losses, to run away and hide, to fight, to give up, and to forget about the battle.

The core of every Scripture is about our complete surrender to God. He tells us through what He has done for others that He is able to heal our pains, bring us out of binding situations, and be glorified in our sufferings.

The issue of control is of utmost importance. Who is in control of me, of my destiny, of my daily walk? Who is in charge of how I spend my time and money, what I put into my body, where I go? Don't I have a say in what I do?

The answer to this is a resounding yes. From our reading of what happened to Adam and Eve, we understand the choice we have as human beings to select our paths and follow them to fruition. But we do not possess foresight to know what events are ahead so we can make decisions according to what the future holds. We do have examples of people who have taken certain paths in the past, and we can infer that we will have similar positive results on the same path. However, sometimes our circumstances are different. Sometimes our results are deadly, even though someone else has narrowly escaped death. "There is a way that seems right to a man, but in the end it leads to death."[5]

A Sad Story

Len Bias, a promising basketball player, was the number-one draft choice after graduating from college. Some time after leaving his parents and celebrating with friends, he met with his eternal destiny. He died in his sleep from a drug overdose. Len did not know that his soul would be required of him that night. Other athletes before him may have celebrated in such a manner and survived, but in this case these deeds ended his life.[6]

"Do you not know that your body is a temple of the Holy Spirit, who is in you, whom you have received from God? You are not your own; you were bought at a price. Therefore honor God with your body."[7] While this Scripture refers specifically to sexual immorality in the body, as the temple of the Holy Spirit we are to be given over completely to God. Allowing a substance into our bodies to alter our consciousness or heighten euphoria is not God honoring, and it may result in the loss of our lives.

The Mind

The renewal of the mind is the second aspect of our surrender spoken of by the apostle Paul. He advises us not to be conformed to the world's trappings. He talks of transformation "by the renewing of your minds."[8] The mind is an invisible force in all of us that is at work all the time. Yet until we see its evidence in the physical, we are not sure whether it is working properly or how it works.

Some of us are good at concealing what we are thinking. We act in one manner while thinking in a totally different way. We are able to fool people, allowing our frustrations and anger to come out in other ways. Some of us tell our friends our problems then go back to the situation with a pleasant face. Some go to the gym and work off anger by punching a bag. Some punish their bodies, eating and drinking too much to drown out sorrows, bringing about momentary comfort. Yet none of these strategies provides the peace of mind we need to sustain us over the long haul.

There is a real need for spiritual renewal of the mind. Thoughts can be either defeating or nourishing. They reflect our image of how we relate to others, our abilities to succeed, and our definition of success. They also indicate our beliefs in the existence of God in the world and His presence in our lives.

Ways in which we conduct ourselves can provide evidence of whether we believe God is with us. A person who makes all decisions without consulting God for direction, approval, disapproval, or acknowledgment would be hard pressed to prove He believes

God has preeminence in His life. A person who thinks the world is out to get him, so he had better get it first might have difficulty showing that he has the peace of God in his heart. A person who thrives on the approval of others, and will do what it takes to earn it at any cost, may find dissatisfaction even after receiving such recognition.

Although all kinds of thoughts may enter our minds, we have a choice of what thoughts we will allow to rule our internal and external lives. Jesus said it is not the act of eating food with dirty hands that defiles us, but what comes out of our mouths.[9] What issues from our mouths is directly related to what is in our hearts, including "evil thoughts, murder, adultery, sexual immorality, theft, false testimony, slander."[10] Clearly the renewal of the mind is of utmost importance for our safety and for peace in our neighborhoods.

Being transformed by the renewal of our minds is not easy. It is much easier to fool people. However, eventually our feelings will come out, either in the way in which we embrace or retreat from those who mistreat us or in the manner in which we handle ourselves around people in various situations.

Pain in the Mind

Christian psychologist William Backus describes the emotional and psychological problems that result from difficult circumstances that come into our lives. He believes these problems come from a "spiritual disease," a subtle slipping away from the Lord due to anger with God that has not been healed.[11] As a result a great divide has come between our souls and God. Life circumstances such as divorce, the tragic death of a family member, challenging issues of parenting, and debilitating illnesses can challenge our faith. Wrong thoughts can change us for the worst if our minds are not renewed daily.

Our minds are not made to hold on to every situation in which we have experienced pain. That is why we must forgive and release these experiences from our minds. The effort to remember every wrongdoing, trial, or difficulty can be readily met by a breech if not dealt with. The breech, which Backus calls a rift in the mind, is characterized by pushing ourselves away from rather than into the arms of God. This may come so subtly that we are unable to see anything has changed at first. However, others around us are well aware, and their first reaction may be "What happened to her? She seemed so happy all the time."

Renewal of the mind is important. Some of the worst situations in which we find ourselves are prolonged by the way we think. Jesus gave us some clues to this need when He said, "take no thought for what you will eat or drink."[12] In the early Christian church, people took this literally and helped one another out, "and they had all things in common."[13] People did not have to worry their minds and could easily trust one another to assist them. This type of care frees up the mind to understand the love that God has for us, thereby shortening the time that we have to entertain thoughts of being unloved and unlovable. In the church today as well it is imperative that we assist one another in word and deed so as not to be a hindrance to our brothers and sisters in Christ and in the world.

We are faced with all manner of messages from people we encounter outside of the church and through the media, whether newspapers, television, or the Internet. It is easy to say that we will refrain from reading or listening to various media in order to keep our minds from the evil things of the world. However, the unseen enemy will launch an attack, whether or not you are listening. What he cannot bring to you through the media he will bring to you through people. Most of us need to work to buy food and other necessities. Unless we are agoraphobics, we will meet with people in some manner or another. Our unseen enemy will use others to plant his messages about our circumstances, relationships, and us. Our job is to allow our minds to be changed to think differently from the world.

The Scriptures speak of our transformation as passing from "glory to glory"[14] as we go from one level of grace to another. This transformation is sometimes noted after long periods of time spent as Christians, when we suddenly notice that issues we had in the past are no longer as important to us as they were. Part of the transformation involves soaking in the knowledge and understanding of the Word of God and learning to apply it to our lives. This is part of relinquishing the control to which we wanted to desperately cling. As we learned we allowed the Holy Spirit to give us a view of life that is godly.

Daily Openness

The choice to allow the Spirit of God to live through us must be made each day as circumstances arise. Eventually it will be evident that a change has occurred. Many times the world notices that we are no longer subject to the lure of self-consciousness, self-centeredness, or self-gratification. The vices we once had—such as drugs, lusts, lying, cheating—are the first to change. But God asks for more. He doesn't only want the outwardly clean-looking person. He wants our motives, our drive, and our reason for existing to be centered on Him. As we come into greater intimacy with Him, we come to be identified with Him more than we are identified with our earthly family, our ethnic group, and our regional affiliations. We come to be known by His name, His attributes, and His ways.

John the Baptist proclaimed to his followers, "Behold the Lamb of God who takes away the sin of the world"[15] and "He must increase and I must decrease."[16] So, too, do we point the way to Jesus in the surrender of our thoughts. Our ways of solving problems will lead the world to the Father through His Son, Jesus Christ.

This is not done with our super-strong minds or a self-disciplined way of life. All the discipline in the world will come short of yielding these results. We need Someone greater than our own efforts to help us surrender daily to God's promptings. We need the Holy Spirit, promised by Jesus Himself as our Comforter, Teacher, Guide, Confessant, and One who empowers. Only the Holy Spirit can help us offer our bodies and change our thinking. God is merciful and patient and loving. Knowing we are frail, He sent the Holy Spirit so that we would be able to enter into realms of holiness that are unimaginable! How blessed we are to be His children. How necessary it is that we realize He knows our weaknesses and can help us. May we become increasingly open to His work in us. May we indeed surrender to His love.

Points to Ponder

1. What areas in your life have you been unwilling to surrender to God?
2. What areas in your life has God helped you surrender to Him?
3. How has your surrendered life helped people around you?
4. What is your present prayer?

Part III – Conclusion

Surrender has to do with trusting that the One who brought us into the light has not and will not leave us without help to do what we need to in order to stand in this evil day. It has to do with understanding our own weakness and our need for the Master, whether for healing (as in the case of the woman with the issue of blood) or to worship (as in the case of the woman with the alabaster box). Each of us must admit that God is greater than we are in strength and love, and that although we have choices, we are responsible for the choices we make.

If we admit our frailties and allow the Holy Spirit to work in us even in the midst of unspeakably difficult times, He will never leave us. On the other hand, if we choose in our limited capacity to strike out on our own, although He loves us, He will not interfere. He will allow us all of the experiences we have chosen and lovingly take us back into His arms if we turn to Him. May we grasp the depths of His love for us in our darkest, most confusing and frustrating moments, in Christ's name. Amen.

PART IV

Preparing for Launch

"And He saw two boats drawn up by the lake, but the fishermen had gone down from them and were washing their nets. And getting into one of the boats, [the one] that belonged to Simon (Peter), He requested him to draw away a little from the shore. Then He sat down and continued to teach the crowd of people from the boat. When He had stopped speaking, He said to Simon (Peter), [Launch] out into the deep water, and lower your nets for a haul...Have no fear; from now on you will be catching men!" – Luke 5:2-4, 10 Amplified Bible, (Grand Rapids, MI: Zondervan, 1995)

Part IV – Introduction

The kingdom of God is very different from our society, which overtly or subliminally teaches us to seek retribution on the one who has hurt us. However, Jesus said to the inhabitants of the kingdom of God that if we are robbed, we should give up more than was taken; if we are struck, we should turn the other cheek.[1] Our society says we should take life by the reigns and steer ourselves to our own destiny. But Jesus described members of God's kingdom as sheep who are navigated by the voice, rod, and staff of their Master.[2] By the Word of God we understand our need to let go of the perceived control we possess by this world's standards in order to please God and to allow His Spirit to guide, teach, and empower us for His purposes. This is what it means to walk by faith.

Author John Ortberg[3] described this faith walk by saying that we need to get out of our "spiritual comfort zones" in order to go on the adventures God has prescribed for our lives. He described Peter's walk out of the ship onto the water toward Jesus as a lesson in courage to take the risk of following

Jesus' directive to "come."[4] The fears we face are often issues in our lives that have come about as a result of what we've seen, heard, or experienced and the conclusions we have drawn. Some are due to the discomfort of change and the disequilibrium of experiencing a new paradigm.

The chapters in this section describe some of the issues we confront that cause us to fear as we attempt to maintain control over our situations. Through the exertion of our own mechanisms we waste time and energy when all the Lord bids us do is follow Him, rest in Him, listen to Him, and fix our eyes on Him. All of our efforts lead only to frustration and futility. But if we learn to truly trust Him, we can follow Him anywhere, even to the deep places to which we are being called.

But what is the deep, and how do we move into it? Some have described it as a place outside ourselves; others have described it as our inner being in which we see the workings of God. In this book, the deep has two representations. The first has to do with moving into position when directed by God. It has to do with having the courage to follow when we are encouraged to do so.

Having recently spent some time on the beach, I was amazed by the movement of the waves onto shore and back out to sea. This movement has the effect of pushing people down gently or forcefully, depending upon where and how one stands. Waves can overpower a person who stands against them. That is what happened to my daughter, who was knocked over into a woman who stood behind her. However, learning how to work with the waves can result in a smooth ride, a gentle movement that relaxes the muscles. We see this illustrated when watching surfers who wait until the waves are upon them and stand on the board just in time to ride rather than be pummeled into the sea.

The second definition of "the deep," woven throughout these chapters has to do with the intimacy to which we are being called by the Father. When moving into the work God has called us to, it is important to be constantly mindful of the One who summoned us. As Jesus said after hearing the reports of the disciples whom He sent out, success in ministry is measured not by the subjection of devils to the prophet, but rather because of where your name is written.

These definitions of the deep are interconnected. Each requires courage because they involve moving into unfamiliar territory. Participation results in greater joy and fulfillment. The ability to follow Jesus results in intimacy with the Father we so badly need. Conversely, intimacy with the Father fuels our ability to follow Jesus to deep places where more souls are awaiting the message of love from our Father. A loving relationship with Jesus Christ fuels all that we aspire to be and do in the kingdom of God. The ability to launch out into the deep would be greatly hampered, if not completely stopped, by not operating in and understanding the love the Father has for us and every other person we know.

Because we live under the world's systems and philosophies and our own personal experiences, we come to the Father with preconceptions and misgivings. This is baggage, which at various points needs to be unpacked so that we can follow Him unfettered. Much of what we have been taught in this world system will have to be confronted and unlearned so that we can grasp what the Father wants us to know. As we search ourselves in light of these words, may we come to a deeper understanding of the love of God for us, His ministers. May we relinquish our own ideas of our roles, allowing Him to reveal Himself to us in ways unheard of in our past, allowing ourselves to be loved as only He can. Amen.

Chapter 10

Baggage: Do We Unpack When We Arrive or All Along the Way?

Therefore seeing we have so great a cloud of witnesses, let us lay aside every weight and the sin that does so easily beset us and let us run this race with patience, looking unto Jesus the author and finisher of our faith, who for the joy that was set before Him endured the cross, despising the shame.[1]

On our last family trip, we had to make many adjustments to the manner in which we used to pack. In the past, we took along more items than were needed in case events did not occur as planned. However, because of new regulations on the airlines due to increased security risks, we found ourselves needing to pack very few "extras." As we were transporting our bags from the car to the airport, it became apparent that, because of the weight and cumbersome nature of the luggage, we had brought too much and needed to pack a little more intelligently. For the first two days of our trip, our muscles were sore from transporting our luggage. We needed to change our packing strategy for the return trip.

As we prepare to go forth in the name of the Lord, we need to be keenly aware of what we are carrying. When Jesus sent forth His disciples to proclaim the kingdom of God and lay hands on the sick, He commanded them to travel lightly.[2] Jesus told them that their work as His messengers would cause people to support them. I believe He gave this reassurance because He understood how easily they could be encumbered on the journey with the temptation to be self-dependent.

A Storage Problem

The metaphor of baggage represents our tendency to store physical, mental, emotional, and spiritual excesses within us. Some of these items may seem harmless at the time they are packed, but they end up being a tremendous weight when we are trying to go through life as helpers of one another.

At the physical level, excesses in what we eat may make us less active and result in a significant weight gain. This can affect our emotional well-being when we are no longer able to fit in our normal clothing or when others refer to us in less-than-flattering terms. Our anger with people for not looking beyond our weight to see a real person with feelings might then be directed at God for making us this way.

Many times, by keeping our baggage of anger, low self-image, shame, and guilt, we keep people from getting too close to us so as to avoid being further hurt. Thus, carrying baggage can be a vicious cycle from which it is nearly impossible to escape.

This simplified example is just one instance in which physical, mental, emotional, and spiritual issues are intertwined. It is not always this easy to define how one has come to have baggage. But in order to travel lightly, there must be conscious thought on a regular basis to decide what to do with these weights. If one haphazardly stores or keeps them too long, there will come a time when overload is experienced.

So do we carry the baggage until we get to heaven or should we unpack along the way? I asked this question of a colleague recently, who immediately replied, "Unpack along the way!" However, providing the logical answer and actually relieving ourselves of these weights are two different things. Before discussing how to alleviate the baggage, let us go deeper into its definition.

For purposes of our discussion, *baggage* is defined as issues in our lives that cause us to distance ourselves from God, call on Him as a last resort rather than a first, and distract us from spending time with Him. The manner in which we deal with these issues may cause God to be angry with us and not want to be in our presence. This reaction from God is not a desirable one for any child of God, for in God's presence is fullness of joy.[3] Even when we are not given answers for our suffering, we are able to obtain an eternal view that allays our frustrations when God is with us. There is no place that is not enlivened, refreshed, and invigorated when God is present. To go through the trials of our lives, we need God to be with us as "a very present help in trouble."[4]

As We Travel

There are varying levels of experiencing the presence of God. God told Moses He would send His angel in front of Israel, but He Himself would not go up "in your midst,"[5] due to their stubbornness. At the same time, God met regularly with Moses on the mountain, giving him specific details about what was ahead. In the same way, we can provoke God to put distance between Him and us through our attitudes toward the issues He allows in our lives. Or we can refuse to worry, electing instead to allow nothing to distract us from intimacy with Him.

Entering

There are two instances of travel in the Scriptures that come to mind as we grapple with the issue of what to do with baggage. In one instance, Israel is entering Egypt. In the second, they are leaving.

In Genesis, the tribes of Israel went to live in Egypt, totally unaware of what lay in their future. Joseph, one of the younger sons of Jacob, had been sold into slavery years earlier by his older brothers out of their jealousy over the preferential treatment he appeared to have received from their father. When he began having dreams of being lord over his family, they decided they had endured enough of him. They sold him into slavery, thinking they were rid of him forever. However, God used Joseph to save the lives of his family years later.

By the time a famine occurred throughout the land, Joseph was in an influential position in Egypt. His role was to store food in anticipation of the coming shortage and sell it to the citizens of Egypt and neighboring countries. When his brothers came to buy provisions and discovered Joseph, their brother, in charge, they received his forgiveness and kindness and their families ended up staying in Egypt.[6] Relieved of the baggage of jealousy, murder, and conspiracy against their brother, they were able to move into Egypt with full confidence that they would be protected.

After the deaths of Joseph and the king under whom he served, the new king felt threatened by their presence. Rather than banishing them from the land, the king chose to enslave the nation of Israel, placing them under hard taskmasters to do the king's bidding.

Leaving

The second instance of travel is recorded in the book of Exodus. God, having placed people in strategic places, set in motion a plan to help Israel to escape from Egypt. In preparation for leaving, God gave orders for the Israelites to wear their traveling garments. Although they packed some things to take with them, they did not pack as heavily as they might have wanted, for they had very little notice when it was time to leave. In the middle of preparing bread for their journey, they had to pack the dough with their clothing.[7] God provided for them on their journey.

Through this story we are reminded that we are not the sole providers for ourselves. God will make ways for us to have everything we need, even where there seem to be none.

The children of Israel carried much physical, psychological, emotional, and spiritual baggage out of the land of Egypt. A first indication of this was the complaints leveled against Moses and Aaron when they were hungry. Rather than being glad they were no longer enslaved, they wished they were back in Egypt, sitting around "pots of meat" and eating "all the food we wanted."[8] After God provided daily food for them to eat, they complained that they were thirsty. "Is the Lord among us or not?" they asked.[9] Despite their lack of faith, God miraculously provided water for these people. He later caused them to win a war against the people of Amalek, who had attacked them.

Our wonderful, merciful God may be angry with us due to disobedience, anger, and shortsightedness, yet because of His covenant with His people and His deep love for us, He will deliver us from horrible circumstances. As His people, we are to unpack as we go through life and travel lightly, not allowing "every high thing and imagination" to set "itself up against the knowledge of God."[10] As we unpack, may we burn up the attitudes and ways that displease God so as to be ready to follow His command.

We Need God's Power

God has provided the sacrifice of Jesus, His dear Son, to be the atonement for our sin. He rose from the dead with all power in His hands.[11] "All power" means power over our imperfections and shortcomings, power over whatever can be imagined. After Jesus ascended to heaven, He sent the Holy Spirit to guide us. Therefore, with full knowledge that we have no power to win victory over our infirmities, we can confidently face what lies ahead in our lives. Now, as we continue to give God our best, we boldly approach the throne of grace and find mercy.[12] We can stand in the power of God, throwing off the unfruitful works of darkness—the burdens and cares—and walk as He commanded His disciples. Jesus told them not to even take an extra pair of shoes or a purse.[13] From this we see that the provisions of God will be made for us so we need not worry about how we will eat or dress. We only need to do as He tells us. He will take care of the rest.

Unpacking involves understanding that everything in this world belongs to God. Even though something is in our possession, we are only stewards of it, so it is not difficult to give up. This does not mean we don't buy clothing or purchase a home in which to raise our families. It means we look at these things not as extensions of ourselves or reflections of where we stand in society, but as tools for our use while we are here.

We also see these things as tools for God's use. A constant prayer of my heart over the years has been that those who enter our home will come to know Jesus personally, that their lives will be forever changed. I expect my husband, children, and myself to share issues of eternal significance with our friends through the way we treat people and encourage our visitors in their walk in the Lord. We pray for issues in their lives at their request.

If we get too involved in owning things, they may begin to own us. This burden of keeping up with neighbors and bearing the trappings of society needs to be discarded regularly. Then we can use these things for the furtherance of His kingdom and shed them at a moment's notice with full knowledge of our temporary state.

Emotional Baggage

Some people are not so worried about owning things, but are wrapped up in emotional issues. This may have begun in childhood or well afterward, when those they trusted hurt them. Some carry the burden of being the family counselor. Like a revolving door, family members come and go, asking their advice and receiving help. However, when they are in need, there is no one to hold, help, or provide wise counsel. They may feel resentment or a need for revenge and carry around a burden of terrible hurts no human being should have to endure. Sometimes, in talking to individuals who do not understand their plight, they become further angered by the apparent callousness to their pain. Wanting someone to pay for these infringements, sometimes they forget that God knows who has taken advantage of or wronged us, and will provide justice for us.[14]

Jesus gave at least one illustration of what would happen to someone who victimized his people. He pronounced suffering on anyone who caused his people to sin.[15] Our rest should go beyond the assurance that God will repay, to the fact that in Him there is complete healing for us. The healing is necessary because as we have heard many a person say after having seen the punishment of their victimizer, the pain does not go away just from seeing punishment served.

Our enemy would like to utterly consume us. He seeks to build up dividing walls between us so that we cannot pray for others or cannot see the hand of God in our situations, and therefore we stay bound up in our own problems without any thought for others. This is the "me" generation, in which everything has to please me before I will entertain it, everything must be to my liking. The gauge of the worthiness of any endeavor in this world has become whether it is pleasing to me. This baggage is toxic. In many cases we are so busy nursing our wounds or seeing to our needs, we are incapable of helping others. We need desperate assistance in unpacking our baggage.

How Do I Unpack?

Unpacking also involves receiving forgiveness, receiving the provisions God makes for us with thankfulness, and embracing Him in our present circumstances. It also involves not allowing anything to be attached to us, not adding anything to our load. Along the road of life, we tend to attract all types of issues, including guilt, anger, pain, fears, and disappointments. Our enemy would love to see us continue to pack on the pounds, so as to devour our faith. Our job is to be mindful of his devices and purposes.[16]

The manner in which we become engulfed in weight bearing can be subtle. Envy, pride, or the unwillingness to forgive eat away at our inner core, changing our view of people in the world, stifling our ability to help others while developing a hard shell of protection. The pain endured at the hands of others is sometimes difficult to release. We are at times hit where we are especially vulnerable, embarrassed, or taken advantage of mercilessly. When the purveyor of pain has betrayed our trust, we want to warn him against any future plans for harm by striking back. Sometimes hearing of others going through similar pain boils our blood and makes us increasingly bitter. This hold will ultimately take root in our hearts, devouring our love and compassion, rendering us unable to fulfill the destiny God has placed before us.

The word *devour* may sound too dramatic, or it could make us think it can be easily anticipated and thus avoided. It is avoidable, but like a spider web, it is often not possible to see the trap. Thus we walk right into entanglements that only the mercy of God can cut through.

Traveling Light

Forgiveness is a two-pronged issue. On the one hand, Jesus said we must forgive if we expect to be forgiven by the Father. So, for our own sakes, we must release others from owing us. Forgiving others so we can be forgiven by God is often a motivation for doing what otherwise is a displeasing act. On its face, we are forgiving in order to receive God's favor. This aspect alone may clarify why many of us still do not forgive. We become so angry we don't care what happens to our relationship with God.

We understand that to forgive others is to remove a burden from the persons who are guilty of wrong-doing toward us. We do not necessarily want this, but instead want them to feel the pain we have suffered at their hands. We feel justice is served by the anger, bitterness, and hatred we inflict on them. Even if it is not obvious to others, we are less than gracious in our thoughts and wishes toward these people.

If we do not forgive the people who have hurt us, it is possible they could repent of their sin to God and be completely free of this debt even though we still feel we are owed. This lack of forgiveness can stunt our growth and hinder our ability to fellowship with God and other Christians.

A regular prayer life and personal Bible study are essential. This sounds simple, but the personal nature of this endeavor includes *thinking*. I remember being in a retreat some years ago and listening to a series of questions asked by a woman who had a psycho-logical impairment. When women answered her, she repeated what they said as if she were gathering recipe procedures. I believe those who follow simpli-fied steps without thought of the One from whom this direction comes may be headed for disappointment. We need to really think about what is being said to us in the Word of God, to allow it to enter into our spirits as water soaks down into the soil of a potted plant.

I believe this process of thinking deeply about God's Word is an important ingredient of blessedness. Psalm 1 describes a blessed man, listing as his delight "the law of the Lord, and in His law doth he meditate day and night."[17] Meditation goes beyond thinking, beyond persistent thought upon God's precepts, rushing from idea to idea and concept-to-concept, as we are so tempted to do in this age of information. Meditation takes internal work, for we are commanded in God's Word to abandon every thought that is contrary to what we know of God.[18]

As we throw down undesirable thoughts contained in the root of bitterness, may we invite the Holy Spirit to plant in us a renewed vigor for this hurting and dying world. May we come to understand the true significance of meditation before God, soaking in His goodness and presence slowly and thoroughly like a sponge in water. May we come to understand what Jesus saw on the cross when He prayed, "Father, forgive them, for they do not know what they are doing."[19]

Points to Ponder

1. How difficult or easy is it for you to identify and release the baggage you tend to pick up?
2. How do you recognize issues in your life?
3. What needs to be released?

Chapter 11

Watching God Work

At one point in my life I was wondering how I would get to the place I believed God had prescribed for me. I was married and had children. My husband and I had good careers. By society's standards we should have been deliriously happy. But I sensed God was calling me into other places. I had an overwhelming heaviness on me, causing me to weep uncontrollably. In my mind's eye I was standing at the bottom of an outdoor staircase, looking down the sidewalk, when God whispered these words to me: "Watch Me work." At the time I heard this I felt as though the floodgates opened. I felt a release in the Spirit. However, only God knew what this would mean in the future. I would like to share with you a small part of what I now understand this to mean.

Watching God work represents the ultimate in trusting God. This trust may manifest at times when there are no other options, or when there appear to be other viable alternatives.

No Other Options

Three nations joined forces to war against the children of Israel with the intention of destroying them. Jehoshaphat, then king, knew that Israel was incapable of winning against these formidable enemies. He was also unable to think of a solution that would have resulted in their victory. Thus, he responded by looking up and proclaiming to God, "Our eyes are upon You."[1] It was understandable that they would look up, for there was no other way to win the battle but to look to God.

We see this response in our world today when we receive dismal news from a doctor and we realize we need someone to intervene on our behalf. We also see this when we go through extreme situations and call upon God as our only hope. During these times our feelings can go from utter hopelessness to resignation to acceptance. Another feeling might be the peaceful understanding that this situation is out of our power to change and it is up to God to deliver us or allow our death. In the latter description, there is a glimmer of hope, which is important to faith.

What is significant to me about bringing issues like this to God is that we have no other recourse but to watch and wait after we have given our request. We can't demand anything of Him or make a case for our worthiness. It is purely in the hands of our merciful and sovereign God, and we will live with whatever is His response, learning to trust that He has our best interest in mind.

What Am I to Choose?

In today's society, there always seem to be options. These choices involve asking questions and thinking through the "what ifs." However, sometimes there is a result that could not be anticipated. The chances of certain things happening betray our ability to choose wisely. We want to know the future before we make the choice. Some choices involve a compromise to one's integrity, but all of them represent taking matters into our own hands at times when we need to release our situations to God.

When we try to handle our own lives, stress increases. This is the opposite of what God wants for us. We must be still, allowing Him to work on our behalf, not trying to orchestrate our own deliverance. Sometimes He tells us what to do about our situations, but other times we need to simply trust Him to work out our problems. The time when we must trust without seeing has been termed the "dark night of the soul" by Teresa of Avila.[2] This time of disorientation, when we cannot see or sense the presence of the Father, when we feel all alone, can be discouraging. Yet these are the times, more than any others, when our faith is strengthened. These are the times when our grip on our situation loosens and God is there, even if we don't realize it.

Years ago, my brother, a minister, was teaching Bible class when a woman asked him, "What do I do when I am so burdened I can hardly go on?" She described her weariness at trying to keep everything afloat, unaware that she was the spokesperson for many of us who listened in silent desperation.

My brother's reply was simple and direct: "Whatever is going wrong and can go wrong, let it." He spoke of our need to release our problems to God, who had the power to handle any situation.

The muscles in my neck relaxed. I had also been a person who kept trying to hold everything together so that nothing went wrong. But the minister's response changed everything, for I realized I did not have to figure things out, that battles in my life were the Lord's. I came to realize that no matter what was ahead, God was with me to see me through.

When Israel left Egypt, not knowing where they were ultimately going, following Moses out to worship God, they came to the Red Sea. With the Egyptians in hot pursuit, the sea before them, and mountains on their sides, what were their options? They could have turned and fought the Egyptians. They could have surrendered. They could have attempted to scatter out in the desert so that some of them could get away at the expense of others' lives. They could have jumped into the sea, committing suicide to avoid slaughter by the Egyptians. Each of these options would have resulted in further bondage, surrender to fear, or death. Yet God used this situation to show Himself faithful to His people. In essence, He told Moses to forget about any other options and watch Him work.[3] His simple directions could have been met with skepticism, but there was no time. Moses, having recently had some experiences with God, stretched forth the rod in his hand as he was directed and watched events unfold. This resulted in no loss of life among the Israelites and their safe passage away from the threat of the Egyptians.

God's solution always involves our trusting Him. All of us, although we may be reluctant to acknowledge it, are dependent upon God for our very existence and subsistence. However, at times we expend so much energy and waste so much time trying to make things happen the way we wish that we forget Jesus' statement that we are powerless without Him.[4] Are we ready to trust Him in every area of our lives? Are we ready as Moses was, to be the example in doing as God has directed? On that day as they stood at the Red Sea, God's people did not need to fight. They only needed to behold the handiwork of the Father. God not only parted the sea and dried the land beneath their feet. He also dealt with Israel's enemy, destroying the army by burying them under the sea.

Discernment

Sometimes God will direct us to pursue our enemy, as He directed David on many occasions. At other times, He will work miracles before our eyes, as He did before Moses and Israel. These are times when He proves Himself to us by strengthening our ability to trust Him in every situation. Many times we are in situations when every option involves the expenditure of energy. God will let us know whether we should be still or fight. It is our job to listen and obey.

Sometimes our watching is not so much external, but internal. We are to watch the work God does in us, changing our outlook on life from negative to positive. He changes our internal stance toward circumstances from fear to faith in Him. We are convinced on a daily basis that we are His children by His Holy Spirit, and He regularly directs us by giving us desires. We need to trust that He is giving us these desires because we are following Him and watching Him open doors for us to do the work to which He has called us.

"Trust in the Lord and lean not to your own under-standing."[5] As a young girl I heard my grandmother say many times, "My mind don't fool me." She is deceased, but I think of her words often because my human mind is fallible. Fearsome sights before me result in misgivings and wondering whether I should stay or go. If I just went by my own understanding or internal reactions, nothing would ever be accomplished for God. But if I watch God work in my circumstances and my heart, I can do great things for the kingdom.

Quietness

One of the most powerful activities we should engage in is a study in quietness.[6] Quietness involves a cessation of the clamor of daily activities, turning down the volume of life, and tuning in to God. Being still, yet standing firm on God's promises. It is a time to gather strength and courage. When God speaks to us in quiet times, we become more focused. Many of the early saints were contemplative, spending long periods of silence before the Lord. The Unknown author of *The Cloud of Unknowing* describes the life of the contemplative.[7] This life, in my opinion, is the bravest.

The contemplative person gives up the fight with the outside world in order to reach out to God. She or he approaches God with the loving longing placed in the heart by God. She or he does not try to make anything happen, as God in His sovereignty speaks at will in life's circumstances. When He addresses the situation, peace abounds. When He opens His mouth, the earth shakes and mountains melt. Oh, what we miss when we try to do all the talking and none of the listening. There is no need to overwhelm our situation and ourselves with complaints.[8] Instead, let us pray as did the early church, and wait for His empowering results. [9] The Scripture says, "After they prayed, the place where they were meeting was shaken. And they were all filled with the Holy Spirit and spoke the word of God boldly."[10] When God directs, may we be so in tune with His instructions that we can step out as the Lord shows us that the battle is His. May we be among those who understand what the Scriptures mean and can hear what the Holy Spirit says.[11] Amen.

Points to Ponder

1. What makes watching rather than solving difficult for you?
2. What is the longing of your heart?
3. From what obstacles do you need to free yourself in order to hear what the Holy Spirit is saying?

Chapter 12

Into the Deep

"So too the Holy Spirit comes to our aid and bears us up in our weakness; for we do not know what prayer to offer nor how to offer it worthily as we ought, but the Spirit Himself goes to meet our supplication and pleads in our behalf with unspeakable yearnings and groanings too deep for utterance."[1]

Most Christians are not satisfied with a superficial relationship with the Lord. It is part of our nature as the blood-bought children of God to be grateful to Him for bringing us "out of darkness, into the marvelous light."[2] Thus, we say thanks to Him all the time. We spend countless hours worshipping Him, for He deserves everything that is in us. Some aspects of worship take place in the company of other Christians. However, the bulk of our worship is spent one on one with Him, in our quiet devotional times that invigorate us to serve both in the church and in the world. Worship extends far beyond the songs we sing. It involves giving of ourselves to our heavenly Father in every aspect of our lives.

We ask the Lord, "What is it that You would have me do?" The practical answer is that we must do whatever is assigned to us and assist others where we can. In addition, each of us yearns to be exactly where God saved us to be. But sometimes the place to which He has called us, or persons to whom He has called us is not apparent. Thus, much time may be spent asking and waiting for the answer.

The Main Thing

It is natural to yearn for something more. But that something more is not necessarily a prize at which we should be grasping. I believe we inwardly yearn for what God put there—a deep relationship with the Father and Son—and that this can only be attained through the Holy Spirit. Many of us are so relieved God saved us out of darkness that it is possible to spend our lives rejoicing on the shoreline, never to step out into the deep to see what other marvelous things He has in store for us. It is imperative that we not ignore the deep yearning. Instead we should follow him to deeper intimacy with the Father.

In the Scriptures, before God brought our fore-bears into their life's calling, we see instances of His calling them to a greater familiarity with Him. Moses[3] committed murder and ran away from Egypt when he discovered that someone saw him do it. Yet even then the hand of God was preparing Him to lead His people out of Egypt. He lived away from his kin for forty years, but when it was time, God caught his attention and sent him back to Egypt. God orchestrated his marriage into the family of Jethro, the exact place he needed to be in order for him to be called for his mission.

The things Moses did let us know he was human. He learned a great deal about God's mercy and forgiveness. He also learned a great deal about our Father, for he came to understand what a covenant was, and he knew that God was true to His word even when His people did not do as He desired.

For many of us, a lot of living takes place between the call to salvation and the realization of the ministry to which God called us. We must not think that our life choices are all a mistake or try to short-circuit our lives to get to the calling before it is time. God gives us time to get to know Him in real ways so we can weed out things that are not like Him. He allows time to love and trust Him in the mundane and adventurous periods of our lives. God knows we need time. We need moments to understand our lives in Christ, to learn of Him, and to recognize His voice in various situations.

For some, the call to ministry is as dramatic as that of Saul on the way to Damascus.[4] One day we are doing our own thing and the next we are proclaiming the gospel for the Lord. Others of us come upon our work through the practical, and proceed to it as if it was always there for us. In both of these experiences, relationship with God is crucial.

Christ's only directive to the disciples was to "follow me."[5] That is such a simple command, but one that not everyone is willing to heed. The disciples dropped everything to follow Jesus. Jesus was the glue that held them together, teaching them, telling them in secret the revelation of the parables He taught, giving them power to proclaim the gospel and heal while He was here on earth. Yet the call did not seem to solidify in their hearts until after His death and resurrection.

While the disciples were wondering what to do after the crucifixion and resurrection, Peter proclaimed, "I am going fishing."[6] The others agreed and went out into the boat with him. After working hard to catch fish, someone called from the shore, "Have you caught anything?" They responded that they had not. Then they heard the directive that would change the course of their lives. "Cast your nets on the other side of the boat and you will find some."[7] When they did, what a harvest they reaped!

They must have remembered a similar experience when they had worked all night to catch fish and Jesus told them to "launch out into the deep, and let down your nets for a draught."[8] Peter, a seasoned fisherman, had responded, "Lord, we have toiled all night [exhaustingly] and caught nothing in our nets. But on the ground of Your word, I will lower the nets [again]."[9] When they obeyed the Lord even in their exhaustion, they brought in so many fish their nets began to break.

This time, when they obtained the same result, John knew immediately "It is the Lord!"[10] When they came to shore dragging their catch, Jesus was already cooking fish on an open flame on the shore, and He directed them to bring more fish to cook.

In this work of Christ we see the sufficiency of God to provide for His ministers. He knows where the fish are. When we try of our own accord to provide for ourselves, the result is often exhausting. However, when we give ourselves wholly over to Him, allowing Him to direct us, the result is awesome. We ought to trust Him for everything, for He knows what we need even before we pray. Sometimes we become impatient and try to do what we can to make ends meet. Yet God will bless us abundantly when we allow Him to lead us. We don't need to coax Him or try to make deals. We need to rest. Rest in His calm assurance that "I will never leave you nor forsake you,"[11] that "I am with you even to the end of the world,"[12] and "My God shall supply all your needs according to His riches in glory by Christ Jesus."[13]

Fear of the Known and Unknown

We are sometimes hindered by the practical needs to provide for our families. God will allow us to work, but we should not see our work as the sole and primary provision for our needs. That can hinder our ability to move out into areas to which God is really calling us. This issue is an area we need to relinquish to the Father. It is high time we came off the shore at Jesus' bidding and launched out into the deep.

Sometimes we do not heed out of fear. We don't know what is out there. We know our feet are on solid ground if we stay on the shore, but out there, who knows? Fear of the unknown has plagued man in every walk of life. Yet some of the most admired persons stepped out because of a directive, not knowing what was next. The late E. V. Hill,[14] a notable pastor, told how a woman in his church encouraged him to go to college. She gave him as much money as she had, but when he arrived at the college, he had no money for tuition, room, or board. God provided for him through scholarships, and he completed his college education. Stepping out into the unknown may have been intimidating; however, had he stayed at home asking for further direction, he would not have realized a dream which rendered him able to tell that wonderful story about God's provision.

This part of our Christian walk is difficult for many of us. It may seem safe to find a job in the church among the saints. If that is what you are called to do, wonderful! However, many of us hide in the church or among fellow believers because we feel safe there despite all of our imperfections. Our brothers and sisters know our vulnerabilities and pray for us and love us. We receive affirmation from our spiritual kin. However, if the Spirit of God brings about restlessness in your spirit, will you follow? I encourage you to allow the Lord to take you into a deeper intimacy than you have ever known. Let God take you aside and explain what the world cannot perceive. Bask in His mighty presence and then go forth, knowing that you can and must return repeatedly to His wonderful presence for renewal, reaffirmation, rest, and revival.

After the fishing expedition, the disciples ate the fish the Master had cooked. Jesus asked Peter, "Do you love me?"[15] Three times He asked Peter that question, and three times Peter answered affirmatively. As there is nothing hidden from the Master, may we be able to answer affirmatively as did Peter. May we love Him, keeping His commandments. May we heed the call to the deep and go forth, proclaiming His truths to the nations. Amen.

Points to Ponder

1. What kinds of discouragement have caused you to want to return to a former vocation or remain in a safe one?
2. How are you renewed in your call to minister?
3. Where is "the deep" in your life?

Chapter 13

Can God Trust Me?

When Satan was seeking a worthy opponent on the earth, God offered Job.[1] Satan made Job's life the kind of nightmare that most human beings wish would never happen to them. His body was struck with terrible boils, his riches were diminished, and his children were killed. As if this were not enough, Job's community began to judge him wrongly and his wife advised him to curse God.

The major portion of the Book of Job is dedicated to conversations he had with community members and God. As Job's discourse proceeded, it was evident that much of his confidence in his ability to follow God was somehow tied to his own activity. He spoke of his stand in the community and the respect he had possessed among men. He had been quite confident, for every day he made sacrifices to God on behalf of his children. When his children were all killed at once and his estate was reduced to very little, he had many complaints about his treatment. This experience gave him a greater understanding of God and His loving ways, which extend far beyond any activities in which we may engage in order to please Him. He learned of the expansiveness of God and His ultimate sovereignty that is tempered with love.

Many of us have had similar experiences in our Christian walk. We are elated when God shows us mercy and brings us into the kingdom. We have a healthy prayer life, and God is blessing everything we touch. We feel almost like we have the "Midas touch." We open our mouths with confidence about what God *can* do and what we know God *will* do. Then one day, just as we are becoming comfortable, the bottom drops out of our lives. Some person we thought would never disappoint us does so in a big way. Our strong bodies we thought were invincible become ill. Our investments are eaten up by a faltering economy. We're set on a frightening course. All those times when we knew what to do did not prepare us for this devastating experience. For a while we are brave, and like Job we say, "Blessed be the name of the Lord."[2] We remember the Scripture that says, "In everything give thanks, for this is the will of God concerning you."[3] We put on a happy face and try to weather the storm. We watch for a signal that changes back to normal or for the better are near. We console ourselves by hoping for an improvement over what we had before. Every message we hear in church seems to be to us. "Weeping may endure for a night,"[4] "Our light afflictions are but for a moment,"[5] "God is faithful, not allowing anything to overtake us but such as we are able to bear."[6] We hear these words and the tears flow in thankfulness that this trouble won't last forever. Yet when we go home at night, we are in pain. The end of our affliction is taking too long! We pray, "When, O Lord, will my change come? What, O Lord, am I supposed to learn from this experience? Help me to learn it soon!"

Patience

Patience is a jewel in the life of every Christian. "With patience you possess your soul."[7] "Let patience have her perfect work."[8] Without the ability to wait for God to work in us what is His good pleasure, we risk remaining in the shallow end of life, never coming to know and love God to the depth that He desires and to which our souls have been longing. We risk dying without fulfillment of our earthly purpose. To some this might sound too intense, but to those who are "the called according to His purpose,"[9] this is everything. At the end of your life, whether in comfort or discomfort, poverty or opulence, the utmost cry in our inner beings is to learn from our heavenly Father all that He desires of us and to walk therein.

One aspect of patience that sometimes escapes me is stillness. Sometimes in my race to be healed, to smile again, and to be free of a binding situation, I run at top speed through my experiences, not noticing God at every place along the road. Yet this is the ultimate call of the believer. "Take my yoke upon you and learn from me," said Jesus.[10] It is not possible to learn all that is needed while galloping through life's obstacles at the speed of light. Sometimes we need to stop running, open our eyes, and see God in the poor, in unexpected situations, and in His provisions. We need to hear His wonderful words of comfort springing up in our very being. We need to hear His silence in dry places and the quiet message to rest in Him. We need to feel His sadness during our pain, His confidence in our afflictions, and His guiding eye all along our path.

Prepared for Destiny

In light of all the pain we experience, we wish we could just shrink into a comfortable cocoon of existence. But we cannot withdraw forever, for Jesus told His disciples, "No man putting his hands to the gospel plow and looking back, shall be fit for the kingdom of God."[11] Knowing he was destined to go through the experience of crucifixion in obedience to the will of His Father, that the pain would not be forever, and that the rewards after His suffering would far outweigh the agony, Jesus gave His life.[12]

How else was He able to bear the inimitable weight of the cross? How else does one dedicated to the service of God continue in the face of agonizing pain, confusion, and disillusionment? Through Jesus' example we see the ultimate in surrender. All that He was and came to do were tied up in that selfless act of presenting Himself in our place on the cross. Knowing His Father's will, He did not set out to change it, but to embrace it. On that day, He placed all of Himself on the cross.

The pain of what He endured is unimaginable. He was condemned for being Himself and yet was unafraid to publicly proclaim His Father's will. This act confirms the lengths to which He would go in loving His Father. He broke no laws, but He angered the religious leaders of that day to the extent that they did what they thought was right to preserve the social order of the day.

We may likewise have to go to extremes to obey the will of the Father. We are not promised that the world will agree with us. Not even every Christian will support our position. We will not always be encouraged and nurtured.

Despite the lack of faith of the religious leaders of that day, Jesus did His Father's will. This was the one sustaining beacon in a dark place: knowing what was the will of the Father for His life, and following His divine purpose. "For this cause came I into the world."[13] One of His disciples tried to convince Him not to go to Jerusalem to die. Yet that was His destiny.

What is your destiny? Are you hurtling through your life, sure of your relationship with the Father but unsure of the work to which you are called, thus feeling ineffective? Or are you following the path of least resistance, making no difference in the lives of others? Perhaps you are among the few who will not be satisfied with the way everyone else does it and are seeking God for all that He has for you.

Are you a marathon runner, prepared to be in the race for the long haul, pacing your steps and being aware of your surroundings? Are you a hurdle jumper who has established a rhythm to your steps that prepares you for each obstacle? Or are you a relay runner, keeping your hands dry and your pace ready, so that when you receive the important message, you may carry it to the completion of the race? Each of these runners has traits Christians would do well to emulate. Each must be prepared for the race ahead.

Blessings in the Here and Now

The Word of God prepares us mentally and spiritually for the road ahead of us. However, Job teaches us that trials benefit us. They give us more definition and more focus on our destiny. They are spiritual exercises, helping us to be more attuned to the voice of the Master. To stop moving toward a difficult experience is to stunt our own growth, limit our learning, fail to be all that God has called us to be, and to come to the end of our lives unfulfilled.

"Wherefore seeing we have this ministry we faint not."[14] The words of the apostle Paul ring true today. Trials in life may seem to come only to wear us down, but God allows discouragements and tribulations in our lives to strengthen us as purveyors of His Word. This is evident in many of the great persons of faith in the Holy Scriptures and in today's society.

Just as the disciples followed Jesus for three years before assuming leadership roles in ministry, preparation for ministry is necessary, and only God determines when you are truly ready. God may draw you away as He did Moses, as he was tending the livestock for his father-in-law in Ethiopia. There on the backside of the desert, God called him to attention. There was Moses, ready for service, but still doubting his ability to lead God's people. God, in full knowledge of his readiness, allowed Moses to take his brother to help him deliver the message to Pharaoh. This is a wonderful testimony to the graciousness of our God, who places within us the void, prepares us for ministry, and fills that emptiness by bringing us forth in the work with help at our side.

From Servants to Friends

Not everyone is ready to carry God's Word. When Jesus chose His disciples before He sent them forth, He instructed them. They became believers in Him, listened to His teachings both publicly and privately. To them He revealed His Father's plan. They had intimate knowledge of Jesus, His ways, and His Father's ways. He taught them with full knowledge that one of them would betray Him and never carry His Word. As their coach, he had direct supervision over them in terms of what they were to proclaim, what they should wear, how they should greet people, and what they should carry on their journey. Jesus continually taught and sent them out, giving them practice for the road that lay ahead when He would no longer physically be with them.

The words Jesus spoke to them became increasingly intimate. At one point, as He revealed His Father's will to them, He said He no longer considered them servants at the level of children. They had become His friends with knowledge of the plan of salvation, of His place in this plan, and with open hearts for the coming of the Holy Spirit. Even though they each had weaknesses and an incomplete understanding at the time of this discourse, Jesus planted a seed that would germinate and later come forth when they were empowered by the Holy Spirit.

God will give us full knowledge when He wants us to go forth. He will take us into His bosom and coach us through mighty men and women of God, ever bringing us into greater intimacy with Him. He will open the door and allow us to go forth in the ministry, continually guiding us into all truth as we follow Him.

The Scourge of the Enemy

Our enemy's job is to try to stop us from reaching our destiny. He will launch his attacks through well-meaning Christians who don't understand what the hubbub is about. They will try to define you by what others before you have become. They will question your every weakness. Satan will attack your thought processes as you sift through the junk thrown at you. He will send unbelievers to attack your ability to grow toward Christ through shameless offers of power, influence, and position.

Yes, the enemy is out to devour you, to swallow up whatever God is trying to birth in you before you even become pregnant with the seed of the ministry to which you are called. Because of the need for preparation of the womb before the seed is planted, the enemy will try to prevent the implantation, to force a miscarriage. Just as the enemy tried to end Jesus' life when He was young by causing Herod to order that all male children under the age of two be killed, so will the enemy try in the early stages of your ministry to stop you before you even know what your destiny is. But God, in His infinite power, will not allow His work to be forever delayed or ultimately thwarted. He will bring you forth at the proper time to step into your destiny.

Your enemy does not stop after your destiny has been fixed in your view, nor once you have stepped into your calling. We see this in the life of John the Baptist, who at the end of his ministry sent to Jesus his questions of whether He was in fact the Christ. Satan's job is to affect discouragement whenever He can, because our faith in the Father through Jesus Christ is intimately tied to our destiny.[16]

Those who would deceive you by saying you can't lose your way after you have found your destiny only deceive themselves. What is the answer to the conundrum of faith and destiny? It is to walk by faith and not by sight, ever seeking to walk intimately with the Father in our life's calling.

When we become caught up in the work and forget about the One who called us to that work, our faith is endangered. As we carry God's precious Word to a dying world, may we continue to seek His face, for in Him is eternal life. May we who are entrusted with the Word of God and His glorious ministry ever walk in His blessed light. Amen.

Points to Ponder

1. In what areas of your life are you discouraged?

2. What effect has this discouragement had on your faith in God?
3. What is your inner yearning toward God regarding your role in carrying His Word?

Chapter 14

Pressing Forward

Brethren, I count not myself to have apprehended: but this one thing I do, forgetting those things which are behind, and reaching forth unto those things which are before, I press toward the mark for the prize of the high calling of God in Christ Jesus.[1]

Stagnancy is the enemy of the soul. The tendency to rejoice over a victory may lead to complacency, which spells danger. The reason for this danger is the convoluted way in which the enemy of our souls attempts to distract us from our main focus.

The Right Focus

As we walk into our call in life, the level of comfort experienced is phenomenal. The burden we have for the people with whom we fellowship and among whom we have leadership in the Lord is inescapable, undeniable, and keeps us working consistently with little or no earthly reward. It is gratifying to see a person growing in grace, being healed, being delivered, or understanding how to walk before God. However, we should never be so caught up in the work that we lose our focus, for the work may become tiring. People may not respond as they had previously. Even though it is important to gauge the effectiveness of our work among people, our lives cannot be solely centered on the response of those to whom we are called to minister. Life has to be about Someone higher.

When His disciples came to Him, rejoicing because demons were obedient to them, Jesus cautioned them against rejoicing over this power and reminded them that the focus of their joy should be because their names were written in heaven.[2] Knowing how the joyful immediacy of a circumstance can sometimes make us giddy, Jesus provided the real focus for which our enemy is constantly contending.

What does this mean for those who are seriously seeking God's direction regarding ministry and life's choices? Why rejoice because our names are written in heaven and not because of the subjection of demons under our feet? To understand this truth, consider what happened to the disciples later in their field work for the Master. They eventually met up with a man whose son had a demon, and they were unable to cast him out.[3] I believe that if Jesus had not refocused them in their earlier experience, they could have easily become skeptical of their calling or Christ's ability to empower them rather than just confused as to why they were unable to free the child from the evil spirit.

When we focus on our work rather than the One who called us, we can become complacent or arrogant when the response is good, confused when circumstances seem to deny our calling, or frustrated when life becomes difficult. Times will come when there seem to be neither rhyme nor reason to our lives, and as a result, we may feel as if we should give up. A lack of focus on Jesus can cause us to stop following, stop seeking, and stop wanting to be like Him. That can lead to stagnation. Instead what is needed is openness to the Holy Spirit in whatever circumstances we find ourselves. We need continuity of fellowship with God.

A Continuous Flow

A stagnant body of water soon becomes stale and will eventually smell foul because of the lack of flow of dirty materials out and the deficiency of an inflow of fresh water. So it is with the one who is not refreshed by the power of the Holy Spirit. We endure the chastening of God when we are found lacking in some area of our lives. Not opening up to God to release that which is unacceptable to God and to receive his fresh anointing will lead to dormancy. This will stall our growth in the Lord and thus hinder our ability to hear from Him and effectively minister in whatever capacity He has called us.

God, in His rich mercy, knows our shortcomings. He knows what our enemy will do to try to sidetrack us. Knowing this, He allows us pain at times, whether in the flesh, as experienced by the apostle Paul, or in another manner of difficulty. He allows this pain so we will remain humble and thus open to hearing God's voice.

Sometimes, in our pain, we ask for deliverance. In Paul's case, God's answer each of the three times He asked for healing was "My grace is enough for you. For my strength is made perfect in weakness."[4] In our weakened state, God's strength is doing the work, and the power of God is at work in us. We are free to continue to focus on the Father and allow the work to be done in us, through us, and for others and us.

Almighty God can perform a mighty work in our lives in the midst of our weakened state. May we remain in a dynamic relationship with our Lord, in Jesus' name. Amen.

Points to Ponder

1. Where is your focus?
2. Is your life dependent upon a relationship with the Father in the name of His Son?
3. How is your relationship with the Father reaffirmed?

Chapter 15

Persistent Seeking

When I was a newborn Christian, I was much like the Word of God admonishes us to be. I was desirous of a deeper walk with Jesus right away. During a revival I attended at ten years old, when the minister asked how many of us wanted more of Jesus, I raised my hand so soon after receiving Christ as my Savior that the minister thought I did not understand my salvation. Someone behind me told me to put down my hand, and eventually I did.

For a long time after that, I learned about our Lord and His ways through the preached and taught Word of God. I was satisfied with that initial experience, and others along the way, but the Lord let me know that He had more for me.

Thirty years later, as I sat in a Sunday school class, the memory of my upraised hand wafted back into my consciousness. The Word of God accompanied that memory: "Blessed are those who hunger and thirst after righteousness, for they shall be filled."[1] I rejoiced in my spirit. I knew I was embarking upon something powerful, and it was all because God would not allow the hunger He placed in me to die. During that thirty-year period, I had received both the baptism in water and the infilling of the Holy Spirit, acknowledged my call into ministry, served in many capacities in the church, and studied and received three academic degrees. However, my desire for spiritual growth did not wane. Sometimes I thought I was on the right road because it was obvious I was anointed in what I was doing at the moment. Other times I wished for more, but was not certain what the "more" was.

In recent years I received a conscious movement in the direction in which God was calling me during a study of the book of Philippians with a small group of women. I read Paul's words to the church at Philippi and his prayers for them and how he did not want to be ashamed of them. Those words tore into my soul, for that was the basis of a mask I'd worn for many years. I did not want to be ashamed or embarrassed in any area of my life.

As a result of my realization that I had been hiding, I wrote *Confessions of a Fraud* in my journal. With my life laid bare before Almighty God, I listed everything I had tried so hard to achieve, including perfection in marriage, healthy and well-adjusted children, a well-wrought professional life, and a superior spiritual relationship with God. I understood that I needed God to help me in these areas. I was not thinking that I had accomplished these things, but I wondered about my motive for wanting all these things to be perfect. Sure, I said I wanted them for God's glory, but there was an internal sigh of relief when things went well because I did not wish to be ashamed.

Since that revelation, I have experienced a trial in each of these areas, and I came to see that my spiritual life was still growing. Perhaps my desire for perfection was more about how I looked to others and less about glorifying God. I came to know that each of my shortcomings, failures, and weaknesses was a reminder of how strong God is, for He guided me and still directs me during rough times.

Spiritual Vacancy

God has a way of making us aware of our emptiness. "Apart from me you can do nothing,"[2] He said to His disciples. "Abide in me and I will remain in you. No branch can bear fruit unless it remains in the vine. Neither can you unless you remain in me."[3] This seems such a passive statement, yet in our lives of so much activity, our utmost job is to stay connected to Jesus so we can bring forth fruit. Our life circumstances may become difficult, making us want to let go and give up. Yet Jesus admonishes us that no activity, no motive, and no desire apart from Him are of any eternal significance. The struggle against the forces of the enemy is not about His efforts to make us stop doing anything external, but about our internal relationship with the Father.

Our enemy knows that if we lose our spiritual connection to Jesus, we could keep going through the motions in an effortless manner, like a car on cruise control. Satan knows if he can cut that tie, making us focus on ourselves instead of Jesus, making our relationships with others our center rather than Jesus Christ, we can keep up our activities out of obligation without substance and will eventually crash. We would keep doing good works because they give us satisfaction rather than because they please God. He can deceive us as he deceived Eve at Eden, her son Cain, and countless others.[4]

I have come to the conclusion that my motives, desires, behaviors, thoughts, and activities must all be brought into subjection of Jesus, the Savior. None of these things brings forth fruit without the nourishment of a strong connection to Jesus. It is important to continue to spend time in His presence and to pray for Him to enter into every aspect of our lives.

I Understood as a Child, I Thought as a Child[5]

I thought the Christian experience was something that, once attained, was to be treasured and kept like a lock of hair clipped from a baby's head and preserved in a locket. I thought I would come to a point in my life where I would remain the same satisfied person, doing whatever it was I was made to do, then someday go home to be with the Lord. I admired older Christians, especially how comfortable they appeared to be in their lives. As I have grown older, I realize that the way they appear is a result of their connection with Jesus, and that connection is dynamic and current. It is not static. It is not something that was attained years ago, only to be dusted off regularly and admired by all. It is an ongoing communion with Him. Even though they have known for years that He is their Savior, each day He becomes more, each day He offers more, and each day He imparts more.

I learned this through watching my parents in their most difficult hours, physically ailing and unable to go forth in ministry as they once had. As I engage in discussions with my dad regarding God's ways, and watch my mom's reactions, I see the connection is still there. My dad becomes animated in His conversations about God's Word, and the depth and simplicity of those revelations confirms His abiding presence even in the face of difficult moments.

In this world system, hard work pays off, and we won't have to work as hard when we retire from our labors. The image painted by the world is that we will eventually be able to enjoy the fruits of our labor much like the man in the parable Jesus told who had such a large harvest that he built bigger barns to keep all of it to himself.[6]

Jesus persistently explained through parables how different His kingdom was from the world. He constantly reminds us of how He gives to us to give to others. So a revelation to us is a revelation to others, and an impartation of the Spirit to us is an impartation to others. At a time when the world might view God's men and women as having "arrived" and "accomplished much," old men by this world's standards continue to impart the Word of the Lord, even if they must be carried from place to place. In order to continue imparting to the people of God, an active, dynamic, ongoing relationship with the Father is key, even more than a physically fit body. I have heard sermons from older ministers that have been preached before, but the freshness with which it is preached, the deeper revelation of the same message, is unmistakable. It is living proof that the minister is still continuously in the presence of Almighty God, communing and receiving fresh insight.

What is the message to ministers who are stepping out into new directions in the Lord? There is no greater teacher than the Holy Spirit, as promised to us by Jesus Christ. The depths to which He will take us if we stay connected with Him are inexplicable, even when we are nowhere near where we believe He wants to take us. His mercy, grace, and patience keep us connected to Him. Oh, that we would continue to surrender to His marvelous love!

Points to Ponder

1. What is your experience with the Holy Spirit as teacher?
2. Is your experience always tied to people, or do you spend time alone with the Lord?
3. What is the desire of your heart?
4. Is it clear to you that God gave you that desire?

Part IV – Conclusion

The ability to inspire people to come to the Father through His Son can only be accomplished by those who are in a relationship with Him. My father said something significant to me one day regarding a sales job for which he was being recruited. After he had listened to the script the company wanted him to use to sell encyclopedias, he responded, "What is it about this product that will make me believe in it? If I don't believe in the usefulness of the product, I cannot convince people to spend money they might use for other things in order to buy these books. I can't sell it unless I believe in it."

This is what God has been saying to us as ministers of the gospel. The message is simple, yet profound. Jesus taught us by His example how important it is to be in an honest, intimate relationship with the Father. He demonstrated His honesty when He said to the Father in the garden of Gethsemane that the cup was too hard for Him.[1] He also spoke of the intimacy He had with His Father when standing outside Lazarus's tomb when He told the Father in the presence of

Lazarus's dear friends, "Father, I know You hear me, but that these might know…"[2]

It is impossible to introduce Jesus to a hurting, cynical, dying world if we do not know Him ourselves. We need not only to have been introduced to Him through stories we have heard, but in our own dynamic, life-changing, daily walk. Our lives, however broken they may be, are a testimony to the world of the love of the Father for even someone like us. As we lift Jesus in our lives, others are drawn to Him by this love.

As a minister of the gospel, I have had opportunities to address those who are new to the call as well as seasoned ministers with years of experience. Although I do not consider myself an expert by any stretch of the imagination, my spiritual burden for all ministers has prompted me to write this selection. We who constantly give to others have a great need for our own personal, spiritual revival.

Author Eugene Peterson says ministers need to schedule time on a regular basis to pray, preach, and listen.[3] These essential activities must be engaged in so that we are actively in a relationship with the Father. I believe messages like this, from a pastor who has years of experience, come from the Father, who wants to save not only those who do not yet know Him as Savior and Lord, but also His own servants.

How the Father has been calling the souls of His ministers to melt before His magnificent love! How He longs to spend time with us alone! He bids us come into this wonderful secret place in order to dwell with Him. This means that the most important thing to Him is a relationship with us, in corporate as well as individual settings. God's love is so voracious that Catherine of Siena[4] referred to Him, as "divine madman and drunk with love," much like the lover described in the *Song of Songs*. He loves us so much that, in the midst of a troubled world that needs every man and woman of God to speak peace, He bids us to come aside and rest. He wants to sustain us in this necessary work. He desires to impart more spiritual blessings on us. May we follow with all diligence, engaging in deep, loving communion with the Father by listening and praying, through Jesus Christ our Lord. Amen.

NOTES

Prologue
   [1] 1 Corinthians 9:27

Chapter 1: Down Memory Lane
   [1] Isaiah 59:10
   [2] John 3:19 KJV, *Key Word Study Bible* (Chattanooga, TN: AMG Publishers, 1991)
   [3] Luke 16:23
   [4] 1Timothy 1:15 KJV
   [5] Acts 8:1
   [6] Acts 22:20
   [7] Luke 24:13-35
   [8] 1 Corinthians 15:3-6

Chapter 2: When the Moment of Truth Arrives
   [1] Mae Williams, "Inner Yearnings," stanzas 1, 2
   [2] Luke 15:11-32
   [3] Luke 15:13
   [4] Genesis 3:3
   [5] Genesis 3:12-13
   [6] Mark 8:36
   [7] Genesis 4:26 KJV

Chapter 3: Mercy Suits My Case
   [1] Lamentations 3:30
   [2] Mae Williams, "Destiny"

[3] Psalm 32:8
[4] Genesis 2:16-17
[5] Philippians 4:13
[6] Luke 23:48

Part II – Now in the Light

Introduction

[1] Brennan Manning, *Ruthless Trust*, (New York: Harper Collins, 2002)
[2] Hebrews 4:15 KJV

Chapter 4: Now We Are Light

[1] Mae Williams, "Inner Yearnings," stanzas 3, 4
[2] Ephesians 5:8
[3] 1 Peter 2:2
[4] Matthew 5:6
[5] Matthew 7:9
[6] Ephesians 3:20 KJV
[7] Ephesians 6:17
[8] 2 Corinthians 5:21
[9] Deuteronomy 28:13
[10] Deuteronomy 32:10
[11] Judges 6:12 KJV
[12] Genesis 25:26
[13] Matthew 1:21
[14] Genesis 21:3
[15] Luke 1:5-25; 57-66
[16] 1 Corinthians 4:16
[17] 1 Corinthians 6:20
[18] 1 Corinthians 3:16
[19] Acts 10:9-16
[20] Acts 10:34
[21] 1 Peter 1:17
[22] 1 Peter 2:11
[23] Acts 16:16-40 NASB, *International Inductive Study Bible*, (Eugene, OR: Harvest House Publishers)
[24] Matthew 5:14
[25] Acts 16:28

[26] 2 Corinthians 4:16
[27] 2 Corinthians 5:17
[28] 2 Corinthians 5:16

Chapter 5: The Place of Becoming
[1] Lamentations 3:22-23 NASB
[2] Luke 22:31
[3] Romans 8:37
[4] 1 John 5:4
[5] 1 John 5:5
[6] Hebrews 11:6 KJV
[7] Matthew 9:28; John 8:46; 9:35
[8] Luke 18 27
[9] Matthew 16:13
[10] 2 Timothy 4:5

Part II – Conclusion
[1] Matthew 11:29

Part III – Surrender
Introduction
[1] Luke 8:43-48
[2] Luke 7:36-50

Chapter 6: The Boldness of Surrender
[1] Mae Williams, "Surrender"
[2] Abbe Francois Trochu, *Saint Bernadette Soubirous: 1844-1879*, (Rockford, IL: Tan Books and Publishers Inc., 1985), 104-109.
[3] Revelation 5:8

Chapter 7: The Healing in Surrender
[1] Leviticus 15:19-30
[2] Psalm 122:1
[3] Matthew 11:12
[4] Mark 5:28 KJV
[5] Numbers 15:38; Deuteronomy 22:12; Zechariah 8:23
[6] Numbers 15:39

[7] Mark 5:30; Luke 8:45
[8] Isaiah 55:9

Chapter 8: Surrender to Whom?

[1] Philippians 3:5 KJV
[2] Acts 9:5 KJV
[3] Exodus 20:3
[4] Isaiah 42:8
5 Matthew 7:21-23
[6] 2 Peter 1:10 KJV
[7] Galatians 2:1
[8] Galatians 2:21 KJV
[9] Romans 2:29 KJV
[10] 1 Thessalonians 4:3 KJV
[11] 2 Timothy 2:22
[12] James 4:7
[13] 2 Corinthians 11:14
[14] John 5:39
[15] Luke 10:30
[16] John 14:12
[17] John 11:42
[18] E. Allison Peers, *St. John of the Cross: Dark Night of the Soul*, (New York: Doubleday, 2005)

Chapter 9: The Meaning of Surrender

[1] Romans 12:1-2 KJV
[2] Matthew 5:13-14
[3] Matthew 5:14b
[4] Romans 12:19
[5] Proverbs 14:12
[6] Keith Harriston and Sally Jenkins, "Maryland Basketball Star Len Bias is Dead at 22," (Washington Post, June 20, 1986), 1.
[7] 1 Corinthians 6:19-20
[8] Romans 12:2
[9] Matthew 15:10
[10] Matthew 15:19

[11] William Backus, *The Hidden Rift With God*, (Minneapolis, MN: Bethany House Publishers, 1990).
[12] Matthew 6:25
[13] Acts 2:46
[14] 2 Corinthians 3:18
[15] John 1:29
[16] John 3:30

Part IV – Preparing for Launch
Introduction

[1] Matthew 5:39
[2] John 10:27
[3] John Ortberg, *If You Want to Walk on Water You've Got to Get Out of the Boat*, (Grand Rapids, MI: Zondervan, 2001).
[4] Matthew 14:25-31

Chapter 10: Baggage...Do We Unpack When We Arrive or All Along the Way?

[1] Hebrews 12:1-2 NASB
[2] Matthew 10:9-10
[3] Psalm 16:11
[4] Psalm 46:1
[5] Exodus 33:3
[6] Genesis 41:37-45, 15
[7] Exodus 12:34
[8] Exodus 16:3
[9] Exodus 16:7
[10] 2 Corinthians 10:5 NASB
[11] Matthew 28:18 KJV
[12] Hebrews 4:16 KJV
[13] Luke 10:4
[14] Romans 12:19
[15] Luke 17:1-2
[16] 1 Peter 5:8
[17] Psalm 1:1-2
[18] 2 Corinthians 10:5
[19] Luke 23:34

Chapter 11: Watching God Work

[1] 2 Chronicles 20:12
[2] E. Allison Peers, ed., *The Life of Teresa of Jesus: The Autobiography of Teresa of Avila*, (New York: Doubleday Dell Publishing Group, 1991).
[3] Exodus 14:13
[4] John 15:5
[5] Proverbs 3:6
[6] 1 Thessalonians 4:11
[7] William Johnston, ed., *The Cloud of Unknowing*, (New York: Doubleday, 1973).
[8] Psalm 77:3
[9] Acts 4:29
[10] Acts 4:30-31
[11] Revelation 3:22

Chapter 12: Into the Deep

[1] Romans 8:26 KJV - Amplified Holy Bible, (Grand Rapids, MI: Zondervan Publishing House)
[2] 1 Peter 2:9
[3] Exodus 2:1-4:17
[4] Acts 9
[5] John 21:22
[6] John 21:3-5
[7] John 21:6
[8] Luke 5:4
[9] Luke 5:5 AMP
[10] John 21:7
[11] Hebrews 13:5
[12] Matthew 28:22
[13] Philippians 4:19
[14] E. V. Hill, *A Savior Worth Having*, (Chicago: Moody Press, 2002), 169.
[15] John 21:15-17

Chapter 13: Can God Trust Me?

[1] Job 1, 2
[2] Job 1:21

[3] 1 Thessalonians 5:18
[4] Psalm 30:5
[5] 1 Corinthians 4:17
[6] 1 Corinthians 10:13
[7] Luke 21:19
[8] James 1:4
[9] Romans 8:28
[10] Matthew 11:29
[11] Luke 9:62
[12] Hebrews 12:2
[13] John 18:37
[14] 2 Corinthians 4:12
[15] Exodus 2:11-14
[16] Matthew 11:1-3

Chapter 14: Pressing Forward

[1] Philippians 3:13-14
[2] Luke 10:20
[3] Matthew 17:14-21; Mark 9:14-29
[4] 2 Corinthians 12:9

Chapter 15: Persistent Seeking

[1] Matthew 5:6
[2] John 15:5
[3] John 15:4
[4] Genesis 3:1-5
[5] 1 Corinthians 13:11
[6] Luke 12:18

Part IV – Conclusion

[1] Mark 14:36
[2] John 11: 41-42
[3] Eugene Peterson, *The Contemplative Pastor*, (Grand Rapids, MI: Wm. B. Eerdmans Publishing, 1989), 19-22.
[4] St. Catherine of Siena, *Dialog of Catherine of Siena*, (Grand Rapids, MI: Christian Classics Ethereal Library, 2000), 37.

CPSIA information can be obtained
at www.ICGtesting.com
Printed in the USA
FFHW020626130919
54960094-60662FF